The Point of Words

The Point of Words

Children's Understanding of
Metaphor and Irony

Ellen Winner

Harvard University Press
Cambridge, Massachusetts
London, England
1988

This book is printed on acid-free paper, and its binding materials
have been chosen for strength and durability.

Library of Congress Cataloging-in-Publication Data
Winner, Ellen.
  The point of words.

  Bibliography: p.
  Includes index.
  1. Language awareness in children.   2. Metaphor.
3. Irony.   I. Title.
P118.3.W56   1988   401'.9   87-21092
ISBN 0-674-68125-8 (alk. paper)

*For Benjamin, who has already
committed his first metaphor,
but who is as yet
too innocent for irony*

Preface

I have been unable to shake a nagging and persistent attraction to metaphor. As an English major in college, I wrote a thesis on uses of metaphor in the poetry of William Butler Yeats. At the time, I assumed metaphor to be an issue for poets and literary theorists, not for children and cognitive psychologists. It was through my affiliation with Harvard Project Zero that I came to recognize metaphor as a problem for psychologists. I pursued this interest during graduate school, where I wrote a thesis on the development of metaphoric ability in children and the breakdown of this ability in adults under conditions of brain damage.

Eventually, my interest in metaphor expanded to become an interest in nonliteral language more generally. A study of children's sensitivity to a range of nonliteral uses led me to recognize irony as an intriguing contrast to metaphor. Most interesting to me were the differences in how children misunderstood these two forms of language. It occurred to me that the errors children make in trying to understand metaphor and irony reveal two very different aspects of their thinking. Metaphor is a window on children's classification skills, irony on children's abilities to attribute beliefs and intentions to others. And although both forms of language are alike in being indirect ways of communicating, the two forms serve very different ends. Metaphor serves to illuminate the attributes of things in the world, irony to reveal the ironist's attitude about the world.

My purpose in writing this book was to examine how children come to the understanding, so crucial for communication, that meanings are often unstated, and words are often not meant. By comparing how children come to these realizations about metaphor and irony, I hope to have shown that there is no unitary nonliteral language skill, but instead at least two very different skills involved.

Many people have helped me in this endeavor. For years I have worked with a lively research group within Project Zero, initially dedicated to the study of children's comprehension of metaphor, and later also of irony. Although the members of the group have changed as research assistants went on to graduate school or other things, the spirit and energy of the group have persisted. Members of this group who helped me to think about the issues discussed in this book include Janet Andrews, Paula Blank, Robin Bechhofer, Michael Cicone, Matthew Engel, Amy Demorest, Margaret McCarthy Herzig, Joan Kaplan, Sandra Kleinman, Ulla Malkus, Christine Massey, Eve Mendelsohn, Christine Meyer, Mark Miller, Susan Robinson, Elizabeth Rosenblatt, Anne Rosenstiel, Lisa Silberstein, and Wendy Wapner. Other esteemed colleagues in this group include Hiram Brownell, Bruce Fraser, David Perkins, David Swinney, Sheldon Wagner, and Dennie Wolf. Jonathan Levy, a recent participant, has offered especially helpful suggestions from his perspective as a playwright. In addition to her role as member of the research group, Joan Kaplan helped me with innumerable details in the preparation of this manuscript.

Jerome Kagan read an earlier version of this book and offered valuable clarifications about the differences between metaphor and irony. I thank Elizabeth Hurwit, of Harvard University Press, who did a superb job of clarifying my thoughts.

My own research discussed in this book was supported by grants to Harvard Project Zero from the National Science Foundation (BNS77-13099, BNS79-24430, and BNS84-07366). I am grateful to my program officer, Paul Chapin. I would also like to acknowledge the *New Yorker* for permission to quote from Michael Ryan's "Tourists on Paros," © 1983 by Michael

Ryan; and Martin Secker and Warburg, Ltd., for permission to quote from Andrew Young's "A Windy Day," published in *The Poetical Works,* © 1985 by the estate of the late Andrew Young.

Finally, I owe a debt of gratitude to my husband, Howard Gardner, who has been a member of our group ever since its inception, and who has never failed to challenge, provoke, and inspire.

Contents

· Chapter 1 ·

Metaphor and Irony in Communication

Hamlet	How weary, stale, flat and unprofitable
	Seems to me all the uses of this world!
	Fie on't! Oh fie, fie, *'tis an unweeded garden*
	That grows to seed: things rank, and gross in
	nature
	Possess it merely. (*Hamlet*, 1.2.133–137; italics mine)

Horatio	My Lord, I came to see your father's funeral.
Hamlet	I pray thee do not mock me, fellow-student.
	I think it was to see my mother's wedding.
Horatio	Indeed my Lord, it followed hard upon.
Hamlet	*Thrift, thrift,* Horatio: the funeral baked-meats
	Did coldly furnish forth the marriage tables.
	(*Hamlet*, 1.2.176–181; italics mine)

In neither of these quotations does Hamlet mean literally what he says. In the first case he is speaking metaphorically. Like a garden overgrown with ugly weeds, the world is a place where base motives are allowed to overrule moral ones. Hamlet's description conveys to the audience the *attributes* of the world as he sees it. In the second example he speaks ironically. He adopts a pose, momentarily implying approval of the timing of his mother's remarriage because it is economical. Although Hamlet claims to support his mother by providing a justification for her behavior, the very absurdity of the justification reveals to Horatio and to us that he is sickened by the timing of the wedding. Hamlet's assertion that his mother remarried quickly in order to be thrifty functions above all to reveal to us his *attitudes* (grief, anger, disgust, disdain) about the events in his world. (This example of irony was suggested to me by Bernard Kaplan of Clark University.)

Metaphor and irony pervade not only literature but also the most ordinary conversations. Consider the following likely situation. Weary parents at a restaurant try unsuccessfully to keep their cranky four-year-old daughter from throwing food across the table.

Husband She's just too young to sit still at a restaurant.
Wife Things are coming apart at the seams.
Husband This is what I call a peaceful way to spend the evening.

The first remark is literal but the two that follow are nonliteral: the wife's remark is an example of metaphor; the husband's final comment an example of irony.

Nonliteral language requires us to consider statements that are contrary to fact, yet that are on some level true and authentic. The ability to consider the counterfactual also allows us to create fictional worlds, to suspend disbelief and feel moved as we read a novel or watch a play. In this book I focus on how children acquire the uniquely human ability to recognize and understand what is false on one level but true and worth taking seriously on another level. I treat metaphor and irony together because they are the two chief forms of nonliteral language. By juxtaposing them I hope to clarify what is unique about each form as well as what they have in common that distinguishes them from literal language. I also address the question of whether metaphor and irony call on the same underlying abilities or different kinds of competencies.

Treating metaphor and irony together as the two major forms of nonliteral language assumes a principled distinction between literal and nonliteral language. Such a distinction has been contested (see, for example, Gibbs, 1984; Rumelhart, 1979; Verbrugge, 1977), and it has been argued that all language is at base metaphoric. Lakoff and Johnson (1980), for instance, argue that natural language is filled with expressions that we think of as literal but that are in fact metaphoric. We conceive of arguments as wars, theories as buildings, and time as in flight, and such metaphors are generative. "These facts are the bricks and mortar of my theory," for example, is an extension of the theories-as-buildings metaphor, as is "This theory is built upon another." But attempts to treat all language as metaphoric ultimately break down because in rejecting the distinction between literal and metaphoric, theorists are forced to make a similar distinction phrased in different terms (see MacCormac, 1985, for a discussion of this problem). Lakoff and Johnson (1980) in fact are forced to distinguish between figurative metaphors (those that are part of an overall conceptual scheme and are thus generative and "alive") and literal metaphors (those not part of an overall conceptual scheme and thus isolated and "dead"). It is the premise of this book that the distinction between literal and nonliteral language can and should be made.

Literal versus Nonliteral Language

Attempts to demarcate literal and nonliteral language must first distinguish between two aspects of meaning: *sentence meaning* and *speaker meaning*. Sentence meaning is the context-free, literal meaning of the words themselves, the meaning that is understood by a listener without knowing who said the sentence or the situation in which it was uttered (Carnap, 1956; Davidson, 1979; Frege, 1892; Katz and Fodor, 1963). Speaker meaning is the meaning that the speaker intends to convey by means of the sentence (Searle, 1979b).

The claim that sentences have literal meanings which can be specified out of context has been challenged (see Gibbs, 1984, for a review). Searle (1979a) has argued that literal meaning cannot be determined without reference to certain background assumptions not specified by the sentence itself. For example, to interpret the sentence "The cat is on the mat," we bring to bear the assumption, not specified in the sentence, that gravity exists and that therefore the mat is resting on the ground with the cat on top of it. Similarly, Olson and Hildyard (1980) suggest that there is no literal meaning without context. The statement "I'm bigger than you" said by John to Bill means that *John* is bigger; when said by Bill to John, the same sentence means *Bill* is bigger.

It is my belief, however, that these background assumptions and contextual assignments of the referents of the words are necessary only to determine speaker meaning and not sentence meaning (Dascal, 1981; Katz, 1981). On this account the sentence meaning of "I'm bigger than you" does not include the referents of "I" and "you." The truth conditions of a sentence are to be distinguished from its literal meaning.

Moreover, even if one takes the position that there is no context-free literal meaning, one can still maintain a sharp distinction between sentence and speaker meaning (Searle, 1979b). Although certain background assumptions (such as that gravity exists) are necessary to interpret literal meaning, Searle argues, context plays a much more important role in determining speaker meaning, since a sentence can have radically different speaker meanings depending on its context.

It is tempting to distinguish literal from nonliteral language by arguing that in literal language the sentence and speaker meanings are identical, whereas in nonliteral language the two meanings diverge. That is, in literal speech the speaker means what he says and says what he means: the speaker meaning is thus conveyed directly through the sentence meaning. In nonliteral speech, the argument continues, the speaker says one thing but means another: hence, speaker meaning is conveyed indirectly. To understand nonliteral language, therefore, the listener must construct the speaker meaning through inference.

But this argument is problematic. It is nearly impossible to find examples of literal utterances in which the speaker means exactly what he says and nothing more. If I say, "John managed to park the car," I imply that parking the car was difficult to do (Karttunen and Peters, 1975). If I say, "It's raining," to my husband as he leaves for work on a rainy day without his umbrella, I convey not only the fact of rain but also the implication that he should take his umbrella. Surely the above statements would qualify as literal; yet two aspects of meaning—sentence and speaker—clearly exist. Hence, even with literal language, the listener must use inference to construct the speaker meaning (Bach and Harnish, 1979; Gazdar, 1981; Grice, 1975). In brief, speakers always say less than what they mean, and even a literal sentence requires the hearer to use context to determine the speaker meaning (Miller and Johnson-Laird, 1976; Olson and Hildyard, 1980).

Since speakers invariably mean more than what they explicitly say, the distinction between literal and nonliteral cannot rest on whether speakers say what they mean. The distinction must rest on (*a*) whether the speaker means what he says and (*b*) the relation between what is said and what is meant. Let us examine each of these issues in turn.

The speaker does not mean what he says. In literal utterances the speaker means what he says and also means more. In nonliteral utterances the speaker does not mean what he says but instead means something *else*. This is the distinction proposed by Searle (1979b).

I have argued that in nonliteral utterances the speaker does not intend the literal meaning. But what, then, are we to make of a nonliteral utterance whose literal meaning is true? Must we not, in such a case, admit that the speaker intends both the literal and nonliteral meanings? Consider the metaphoric sentence "The crazed murderer is a butcher." Suppose that the murderer was by profession a butcher, in which case the term "butcher" applies truthfully on both a literal and a metaphoric level. Are we forced then to conclude that in this metaphor the speaker means what he says literally? No. Truth should not be confused with speaker meaning. Unless he is being particularly clever, the speaker does not intend to convey both aspects of meaning (even though both are true), but only intends to convey the metaphoric meaning.

Irony can also take the form of an utterance that is true both literally and nonliterally. Suppose a woman replies to the question "How was your blind date?" by saying, "He had nice shoes." Even if her date did have good taste in shoes, the speaker does not intend to suggest this at all. She instead intends to convey only the nonliteral meaning—that the blind date was a disappointment. (I am indebted to Hiram Brownell for this example.)

Thus, cases of metaphor and irony that are true do not force us to reject Searle's (1979b) argument that in nonliteral utterances speakers do not mean what they say. An extension to Searle's thesis is called for, however: the relation between what is said and what is meant also serves to distinguish literal from nonliteral language.

The relation between what is said and meant. In literal utterances this relation is one of consonance, in that the speaker means both what is said and what is implied. The speaker meaning is a clear, logical extension of the sentence meaning, and there is nothing jarring about the juxtaposition of the two meanings. "Take your umbrella," for example, is a logical implication of "It's raining." In nonliteral utterances the relation between the two aspects of meaning is one of striking divergence: what is meant is not a logical extension of what is said and either appears unrelated to what is said (in metaphor) or clashes with what is said (in irony). The two meanings diverge because the speaker does not mean what he says and means only what he implies.

We recognize the implied meaning of a nonliteral utterance because the surface meaning violates some of the principles governing ordinary conversation. Grice (1975, 1978) has argued that conversations are governed by a general principle of cooperation. In being cooperative, speakers are guided by four maxims: of quantity (be as informative as necessary), quality (do not say what you believe to be false), relation (be relevant), and manner (be clear). When an utterance appears to violate a maxim, and the hearer has no reason to think that the speaker is trying to be uncooperative, the hearer assumes that the speaker does not mean what he says but means something very different.

A metaphor violates the maxims of quality if it is literally false; relation, because the speaker refers to something apparently irrelevant and unrelated to the context; and manner, because the utterance appears irrelevant and thus does not seem clear. Irony violates the maxim of quality if it is literally false; it also violates manner, since being indirect is less clear than being direct. The assumption that the cooperative principle is still in force despite the violation of maxims allows the hearer to go on to recognize the speaker's meaning as neither false nor irrelevant nor unclear.

A Brief Comparison of Metaphor and Irony

Although both qualify as nonliteral, metaphor and irony differ in two important respects: function and structure. The functional difference is that metaphor is used mainly to clarify, illuminate, or explain, whereas irony is used to comment upon, usually critically. Thus, metaphor functions to describe, irony to evaluate, though either may do the other peripherally.

A metaphor brings to light certain attributes of an object, event, or situation and thereby conveys new information about it. Hamlet's metaphor describes human behavior as he sees it. The particular metaphor chosen illuminates some aspects of the topic rather than others. The aspect focused on here is disorder or chaos. Had another metaphor been chosen, such as "The world is a desert," the aspect of emptiness would have been emphasized.

New or striking metaphors highlight infrequently remarked upon (or previously unnoticed) attributes of their referents and in so doing they describe the topic in what the speaker considers to be an illuminating way. Metaphors reflect our conceptual system. When we speak of love as a journey ("We've come a long way together"), of ideas as containers ("There's nothing in that notion"), or of the mind as a computer ("He processed the information quickly"), we reveal how we conceptualize love, ideas, and minds—what we think they are *like* (Lakoff and Johnson, 1980). Metaphors that reveal *new* conceptualizations serve to reshape our thought and, because of their descriptive power, are often at the root of scientific theories (Turbayne, 1970). Freud conceptualized the mind metaphorically as an iceberg, the vast submerged bulk as the unconscious, the tip above water as consciousness. And Darwin conceived of evolution as a race in which only the most fit reach the finishing line. Indeed, theoretical speculation and theory building in science would hardly be possible without metaphor.

Irony does no such things. The chief use of irony is not to show what things are like but rather to convey the speaker's attitude toward a situation, and this attitude is almost always negative. Hamlet's exclamation expresses contempt. It does not clarify or explain the situation. Moreover, through the use of irony Hamlet conveys a degree of cynicism and distance: if he has the wherewithal to use irony rather than convey his fury directly, he must have achieved (or be pretending to have achieved) a measure of distance from the events that anger him.

The effect of irony is not only to reveal the speaker's attitudes but also to polarize an audience, whether present or only imagined, into the initiates (those who understand the irony and share the attitudes of the ironist) and the noninitiates (those who miss the irony because they do not share or perceive the attitudes). The ironist forges a solidarity with the initiates. Hamlet's irony has the effect of conveying to Horatio that Hamlet knows that Horatio is capable of sharing Hamlet's view of the situation.

It is because of irony's primarily evaluative and social rather than descriptive and explanatory function that it usually arises in some kind of interpersonal situation (whether between living individuals, fictional characters, or author and reader). It is perhaps no accident that Hamlet's metaphoric utterance, quoted at the beginning of this chapter, comes in a monologue, whereas his ironic utterance is part of a dialogue.

As mentioned above, metaphor and irony can each (but need not) fulfill the primary function of the other. Thus when a metaphor is used to refer to a topic that the speaker has strong evaluative feelings about, the metaphor not only describes the topic in a new way but also conveys the speaker's stance toward it. This stance may be negative (as when Hamlet refers to the world as an unweeded garden), or positive (as in Romeo's "Juliet is the sun"). But when a metaphor makes reference to a topic that the speaker does *not* have potent evaluative feelings toward, no hint of the speaker's attitude is revealed because there is no attitude to reveal. In short, although a metaphor *may* reveal the speaker's attitude, it need not do so.

Likewise, though irony functions primarily to convey attitude, it may also perform a secondary, non-necessary function of description. Suppose that I go to Florida in January and the weather is cold and rainy. I may later use irony to convey the information that my vacation was a failure. "The weather was really great," I might say sarcastically to someone who asked how my vacation was. In this case I not only comment critically and reveal myself as somewhat unflappable in the face of disappointment but also simultaneously describe the weather as bad. When we use irony successfully to someone who does not share our knowledge of the situation of which we are critical, we not only show our attitude but also convey new information about the situation. But when we speak ironically to someone who shares our knowledge of the situation (as Hamlet does to Horatio), we use irony merely to convey our attitude toward the situation. When Hamlet exclaims, "Thrift, thrift," he tells Horatio nothing new about the timing of the marriage. The irony functions *only* to reveal his attitude toward the timing.

Metaphor and irony differ not only in primary function and intent but also in structure. At the heart of metaphor is the relation of *similarity;* at the heart of irony is the relation of *opposition.* The relation between the two aspects of meaning in metaphor is a relation of similarity in dissimilarity. Hamlet likens the world of human behavior to an unweeded garden. Human behavior and gardens belong to very different categories but also bear some analogical relation to each other. In ironic statements the relation between what is said and meant is a relation of opposition between a positive and a negative tone. Hamlet uses a positive trait (thrift—being rational and careful) to mean something critical (being irrational and cruel).

Comprehension of Metaphor and Irony

Metaphor and irony pose very different challenges to comprehension. To understand metaphor it is necessary to understand the elements being linked. To understand what Hamlet means one must know both about gardens—that, if they are not tended, thick ugly weeds spread and make the garden chaotic; and about human behavior—that base motives may dominate nobler ones. One must also be able to see the point of similitude between the two referents being linked. If there is more than one point of similitude, the more points the hearer understands the fuller his understanding. To understand irony it is necessary to understand the situation in which the ironic remark is made: that it is a situation of which a speaker might be critical, and that the particular speaker has reason to be critical of this situation and wants to convey this to his hearers. Thus, understanding metaphor is primarily a logical-analytic task in which the hearer must recognize a match between two divergent aspects of experience. Understanding irony is essentially a social-analytic task, in which the hearer must recognize the speaker's beliefs and attitudes.

The task of comprehending nonliteral language can be divided logically into three steps.

(1) *Detection of nonliteral intent.* At some level, whether consciously or not, the hearer must recognize that the utterance is intended nonliterally: he must realize that the speaker does not mean what he says, and that he means something very different from what he says.

(2) *Detection of the relation between sentence and speaker meanings.* The hearer must discover the relation between what is said (but not meant) and what is meant (but not said). In the case of metaphor the hearer must recognize that the stated proposition bears a relation of similarity to the implied proposition. In the case of irony the hearer must recognize that the stated proposition bears a relation of opposition to the implied one. As with step 1, this step need not be carried out at the level of conscious awareness.

(3) *Detection of speaker meaning.* The hearer must infer the message that the speaker intends to convey, and he does this on the basis of the relation that he perceives between what is said and what is meant. If the relation is judged to be similarity, the hearer must imagine something similar in attributes to what the speaker refers to explicitly that also makes sense in the given context. Or, if both terms of the metaphor are stated, he must recognize the points of similitude between them. If the relation is judged to be opposition, the hearer must transform a positive evaluation into a critical one.

These three steps will be shown here to be differentially difficult for metaphor and irony. For reasons to be explained, steps 2 and 3 are more difficult for metaphor than irony, and step 1 is more difficult for irony than metaphor. Thus, errors in understanding metaphor occur at steps 2 and 3, whereas errors in understanding irony occur primarily at step 1. To the extent that metaphor and irony yield qualitatively different kinds of misunderstandings, the competencies that are used to understand these two forms of language must differ, despite the qualities that metaphor and irony share in being nonliteral.

A metaphor is more easily recognized as nonliteral than an ironic statement because a metaphor taken literally makes a highly implausible statement. No reasonable person could think that Hamlet really means that the world is an unweeded garden. In contrast, irony makes a fairly plausible mistake or lie, two forms of literal falsehood. For instance, Hamlet might have said that the motive was one of thrift in order to lie, to pretend that he considers the timing of the marriage appropriate, or to get Horatio to see it that way. Or he could simply be mistaken, so psychologically blind that he fails to recognize the insensitivity of the timing. But it is difficult to construe how Hamlet could be either lying or erring when he refers to the world as an unweeded garden. In sum, a metaphor taken literally is implausible; irony taken literally is less so. The degree of implausibility should serve as a warning not to take the utterance literally. Hence, children are more likely to avoid a literal interpretation of metaphoric than ironic utterances.

It is easier to detect the relation between what is said and what is meant in irony than in metaphor, because what is said ironically always refers to the context in which it is said. If one understands the situation and the statement, it is usually fairly clear that the statement is roughly the opposite in tone from what the situation calls for. Hamlet refers to the motive for marriage in what he says, and what he means also has to do with the motive. As long as the listener recognizes that the speaker has reason to be critical, he has no trouble realizing that what is meant is roughly the evaluative opposite of what is said. In the case of metaphor what is said is not relevant, on the surface, to what is going on. Thus, the hearer may be unable to discern any relation between what is said and what is meant; or he may infer some kind of relation that was not intended, such as association.

It is also easier to detect the unstated meaning in ironic statements. If the hearer realizes that the ironic speaker is conveying something opposite in evaluative tone to what he says, there is little chance of misunderstanding; the hearer then knows that the speaker means something critical even if he fails to judge the precise degree of criticism the speaker intends. But in the case of metaphor, even if the hearer realizes that the speaker means to convey something similar to what he says, there is still a large possibility for misunderstanding. For example, there are many attributes the world and an unweeded garden share (not only disorderliness, but also physical elements such as soil, grass, plants, and so on). And there are many things that can be likened to seams coming unstitched—not only unruly behavior but also a faulty argument, shaky faith, or something physical, such as glass shattering. If the husband in the earlier example takes the wife to mean that the child is breaking plates, for instance, this would be an interpretation based on similarity but it would be the wrong interpretation in this case. Or he might simply have no idea what she means. In response to metaphor, the hearer can solve step 2 but remain stuck there, as if to say "I know that this utterance is meant metaphorically and know that I am to infer what is meant on the basis of similarity, but I cannot figure out what is meant."

Because steps 2 and 3 are the difficult ones for metaphor comprehension, it is here that errors are usually made by children. Children are unlikely to take metaphors literally; more often they realize that what is said is not meant, but they infer a speaker meaning either not based on similarity or, more commonly, based on the wrong *kind* of similarity. In contrast, it is often at step 1 that children fail in understanding irony. Hence, irony is often taken as a mistake or a lie.

An examination of children's understanding of metaphor and irony forces us to address the question of the relative autonomy of nonliteral language understanding. Does such language comprehension develop independently of other skills or does it build on other aspects of language development or on aspects of cognitive development? I argue in this book that both nonliteral forms require metalinguistic sensitivity, for both require an awareness that one can say something one does not mean, and that one can mean something very far from what is said. Beyond this, metaphor is made possible by conceptual development because it requires the recognition of potential dimensions of similarity. In contrast, irony is made possible by social cognitive development, by the ability to understand other minds, and by the ability to infer the mutual knowledge shared by speaker and addressee. A study of the development of sensitivity to metaphor and irony thus serves as a window on conceptual development and social cognitive knowledge.

Metaphor and irony are equally important domains for psychological and psycholinguistic investigation. Both are central forms of language, which are readily used and understood, and which must be accommodated by any theory of language comprehension. And each sheds light on different but equally important aspects of cognition. For historical reasons, however, considerably more research has been done on metaphor than on irony. Initially the study of both metaphor and irony was undertaken primarily by philosophers, linguists, and literary critics.

Psychologists did not turn to metaphor in earnest until the 1960s (see Honeck, 1980, for a historical review) and are only now beginning to turn their attention to the problem of irony. For this reason more pages are devoted here to metaphor, although I treat irony as thoroughly as possible, in the hope of spurring as much research on this attitudinal, social topic as has been generated on metaphor in the last two decades.

Chapter 2

Philosophical and Linguistic Approaches to Metaphor and Irony

Before considering the research on children's understanding of metaphor and irony, it is necessary to examine more closely the characteristics of these forms of language. In this chapter I briefly describe approaches to the problem of defining metaphor and irony. Instead of attempting a comprehensive review, I summarize the principal theories that have been debated and indicate my own position.

The Study of Metaphor

Traditionally, the study of metaphor was the province of philosophy and literary criticism (Aristotle, 1952a; Richards, 1936; Cassirer, 1946; Black, 1962). Metaphor was often treated as a frill, a deviant, decorative aspect of language—to paraphrase Ortony (1975), very nice, but not really very necessary. Until the 1970s, metaphor was virtually ignored by linguists, psycholinguists, and psychologists.

What scant attention was paid to metaphor granted it only a minor role in language. In Chomsky's (1965) account of language as a rule-based system, figurative language is understood by analogy to "ordinary" language: semantically anomalous sentences, such as "Colorless green ideas sleep furiously," were admitted as metaphorically interpretable, but only by direct analogy to "well-formed" sentences. Although the terminology is different, this account is similar to Skinner's (1957) view that metaphor involves the transfer of a previously reinforced response to a new stimulus which shares sensory qualities with the old stimulus. Both Chomsky and Skinner speak vaguely of "analogy" or "transfer" to account for our understanding of metaphor.

During the 1970s, with the growing interest in the pragmatics of language, linguists increasingly began to consider nonliteral language, especially metaphor (Grice, 1975; Searle, 1979b). Those in the field of pragmatics were forced to turn to the issue of metaphor as it became clear that sentences can be either metaphoric or literal, depending on how they are used. Metaphors are often distinguishable from literal statements *only* through the application of pragmatic principles and *not* through the application of syntactic or semantic rules.

It was also during the 1970s that psycholinguists and cognitive psychologists became interested in metaphor. One of the reasons for psychologists' interest was the realization that metaphor was not a special, atypical form of language, one found primarily in poetry. Instead, metaphor was recognized as a pervasive aspect of ordinary language and as the primary vehicle for language change. According to this view, language is a graveyard for "dead" metaphors. We commonly and unmindfully speak of "an agreement set in *cement*," "a *weak* argument," "a *warm* smile," "a *line* of argument," and so on. Such "dead" metaphors were once very much "alive." They were new ways of saying something. They died because they were used so much that their original literal referents were forgotten, and their continual use is a sign of their semantic necessity (Searle, 1979b). As metaphors die, new ones are born; thus, language is not only a graveyard for dead metaphors but also a birthplace for novel ones. Metaphor is at the root of the creativity and openness of language. We are continually stretching words metaphorically, using words in ways that we have never heard before. Because metaphors are so pervasive, any theory of language comprehension must be able to account for our ability to create and understand novel metaphors.

A second reason for psychologists' growing interest in metaphor was the recognition that metaphors reflect and reshape our basic modes of categorization. Hence, metaphor came to be seen as an essential aspect of cognition. It is not surprising that one of the most often cited books on metaphor published in the 1970s is entitled *Metaphor and Thought* (Ortony, 1979b).

Because of the pervasiveness of metaphor, and the proliferation of dead metaphors in language, we are usually unconscious of the distinction between metaphoric and literal speech in ordinary conversation. The line between metaphor and literal language is fuzzy because as metaphors become overused, they die and lose their metaphoricity. There is no reason to expect a difference in how we process dead metaphors and literal language, since dead metaphors have in effect become literal. The problem for psychologists is to account for our capacity to understand novel metaphors: Is the process of comprehension the same as that used to understand literal language, or do metaphors call on special cognitive abilities?

Some have argued against the claim that metaphors require special cognitive processes since, as discussed in the previous chapter, all language requires the listener to construct a speaker meaning beyond the sentence meaning (Rumelhart, 1979). But it need not follow that this constructive process is the same for metaphor and for literal language. A novel metaphor surprises the listener and challenges him to solve a puzzle by mapping attributes and relations between the stated or implied elements being linked (Gentner, 1983). Literal descriptions do no such thing but simply describe the world in established ways. In the sense that metaphors force us to understand one thing in terms of another, metaphors must elicit cognitive processes not ordinarily called upon by literal language (MacCormac, 1985).

• *Elements and Forms of Metaphor*

At the root of every metaphor is some kind of juxtaposition of a *topic* and a *vehicle*, which are linked by a common *ground*. This terminology was introduced by Richards (1936) and has proven very useful. The topic is the subject of the metaphor, what the metaphor is about. The vehicle is the means by which the speaker indirectly refers to the topic. Linking them together is the ground, the attributes shared by topic and vehicle.

The most explicit juxtaposition of topic and vehicle occurs in *copula* metaphors such as Shakespeare's "Juliet is the sun." Here, Juliet is the topic, sun is the vehicle, and the ground is composed of such properties as warmth, centrality, brilliance, and so on. A metaphor's ground may have many properties and may even shift depending on the context of use.

Any metaphor, no matter what its grammatical form, can be decomposed into topic, vehicle, and ground. Brooke-Rose (1958) classified noun metaphors alone into five grammatical forms. (1) A metaphoric name may be used instead of a literal one ("The *viper* is gone," referring to a person). Here the topic is unstated but it is implied and must be conjured up in the process of comprehension. (2) A metaphoric name may replace a previously mentioned literal name (as in the unweeded garden example, in which Hamlet refers to the world first literally and then metaphorically). Here the topic is unstated but is stated in an earlier utterance. (3) The topic and vehicle may both be stated and linked by a form of "to be," yielding a *copula* metaphor. (4) A metaphor may involve the verb "to make" in which something, the topic, is said to be transformed into something else, the vehicle ("The many years of hardship made his heart into a rock"). (5) Most frequently of all, a metaphor may involve a genitive link such as Spenser's "the eye of heaven," or Yeats's "cloudy leafage of the sky." In these metaphors the topic may or may not be stated (one can say, "The sun is the eye of heaven"), and the relationship between the two terms in the vehicle creates the meaning.

Metaphors are of course not limited to nouns. Adjectives may be used metaphorically ("*tangled* thoughts"), as may adverbs ("to speak *bitterly*") and verbs ("angry words *burned* her tongue"). But when adjectives, adverbs, and verbs are used metaphorically, they *imply* a juxtaposition of nouns and their referents (Brooke-Rose, 1958). For instance, to say, "Her words burned her tongue," is to imply a juxtaposition between angry words and fire; to say, "She spoke bitterly," is to imply a juxtaposition between words and tastes; and to speak of thoughts as "tangled" is to imply a juxtaposition between thoughts and some object capable of getting tangled, such as string, yarn, or hair.

It is not enough to specify that in a metaphor the topic and vehicle are linked by a common ground or similarity. We need also to distinguish between literal and metaphoric similarity. Ortony (1979a) has proposed a useful method: according to his argument, in cases of literal similarity the points of similarity are of high salience to both terms, whereas in cases of metaphoric similarity the points of similarity are of high salience to the vehicle and of low salience to the topic. If the salience imbalance is reversed, so that the properties shared are of high salience to the topic and of low salience to the vehicle, an anomalous utterance results. To illustrate, the statement "Yards are gardens" is based on literal similarity because the ground linking yards and gardens is composed of properties highly salient to both terms (both are plots of land adjacent to houses where grass and plants grow). The statement "The world is an unweeded garden" qualifies as a metaphor because the property of disorder is of higher salience to the vehicle than to the topic. In contrast, the statement "Unweeded gardens are worlds" is anomalous because the ground is composed of properties of high salience to the topic but of low salience to the vehicle: the property of disorder is characteristic of unweeded gardens but not of worlds.

A metaphor invites us to view the topic *as* the vehicle. Because in a metaphor what is shared is more salient to the vehicle, the result is that we notice properties of the topic that ordinarily go unnoted. I will return to this point when I consider the view of metaphor as an *interaction* between topic and vehicle.

Metaphor as substitution for the literal term. Metaphoric language has sometimes been described as a *substitution* for its literal equivalent. "Metaphor," Aristotle wrote, "consists in giving the thing a name that belongs to something else" (1952a, l. 1457). According to this view, Hamlet's choice of words, "unweeded garden," is simply an alternative way of saying something like "a place governed by base and evil motives."

If metaphor is merely a substitution for literal wording, it becomes an optional and therefore superficial aspect of language. Substitution theories treat metaphor as a deviant form of utterance—decorative and contributing to style, but obfuscating clarity. Aristotle seems to have been ambivalent. In the *Poetics* he states that the function of metaphor is to "save the language from seeming mean and prosaic, while the ordinary words in it will secure the requisite clearness" (1952a, l. 1458). But in *Rhetoric* he explains that "ordinary words convey only what we know already; it is from metaphor that we can best get hold of something fresh" (1952b, l. 1410b).

The substitution view is problematic in at least four respects. First, it fails to recognize that a metaphor cannot be entirely reduced to a literal proposition (Searle, 1979b). The best metaphors are open: that is, they have an indefinite number of paraphrases. There is sometimes no way to choose among alternative paraphrases and no way to know when to stop. A metaphor's power, and its meaning, are inextricably related to its open-endedness.

Second, this view also fails to recognize that a metaphoric name does not always stand in for a literal name. Some metaphors function to plug lexical gaps. "Leg" in reference to a table is an example of such a gap-filling metaphor (albeit now a dead one). It has no literal substitute unless we want to offer a cumbersome circumlocution such as "one of the four things that hold up the table."

Third, the substitution view fails to account for metaphors in which the literal and metaphoric name are both stated. For example, when Hamlet says " 'tis an unweeded garden," the metaphoric term (unweeded garden) is actually functioning not as a substitute for the literal term (world) but rather as an *addition,* since " 'tis" clearly refers backward to "the world."

Finally, the substitution view ignores the issue of similarity. This issue is at the heart of the comparison view of metaphor; hence, the comparison view represents an advance over the substitution view.

Metaphor as implicit comparison. According to the comparison view (also usually traced to Aristotle), a metaphor is an implicit comparison of two terms. It is thus reducible to (or perhaps expandable to) a set of similarity statements linking the two terms of the metaphor (Miller, 1979). Proponents of the comparison view usually use as their examples metaphors in the copula form. For example, the meaning of "Juliet is the sun" would be "Juliet is like the sun in the following respects . . ." The meaning of a metaphor is given by an explicit set of similarity statements. A metaphor is thus an indirect way of comparing two elements.

This theory takes us one step further than the substitution approach because it emphasizes the central role of similarity in metaphor. It is nonetheless vulnerable to the first criticism made above of the substitution view: metaphor is not in truth reducible to its literal paraphrase. "Juliet is the sun" is a good example of an open metaphor. Romeo's statement might mean that Juliet is like the sun because she is beneficent, because she is central to Romeo's life, because she is necessary for his existence, and so on. The open-endedness of Romeo's statement is part of the statement's meaning, and this aspect is lost in a paraphrase.

A second problem is that comparison theorists have conflated the claim that a comparison statement constitutes the meaning of a metaphor with the claim that comparison is the psychological process we use to understand the metaphor (Ortony, 1979a; Searle, 1979b). Simply because we make comparisons in our effort to understand Romeo's utterance does not mean that the comparisons are equivalent in meaning to the metaphor.

Metaphor as interaction between topic and vehicle. The notion that a metaphor is more than a substitute for a literal term, and more than a comparison between topic and vehicle, is recognized by the interaction view. The interaction position was first articulated by the literary critic I. A. Richards (1936) and further developed by the philosopher Max Black (1962). According to this view, a metaphor is not reducible to a comparison between topic and vehicle. Rather, the metaphor creates an emergent meaning, one greater than the overlap between topic and vehicle. This emergent meaning is created by the interaction of topic and vehicle, an interaction that works asymmetrically to transform our view of the topic by means of the vehicle.

A metaphor, it is argued, invites us to look at the topic (the principal subject) from the perspective of the vehicle (the subsidiary subject) so that our perception of the topic (but not the vehicle) is altered. Hamlet invites us to see the world as an unweeded garden but not to view an unweeded garden as the world. In the terminology of Black (1962), the topic and vehicle each have a system of "associated implications" (or connotations). Some of the implications associated with the vehicle get applied to the topic, thus altering the topic's system of implications. A metaphor "selects, emphasizes, suppresses, and organizes features of the primary subject by applying to it statements isomorphic with the members of the secondary subject's implicative complex" (Black, 1979, p. 29). One comes to see the topic as having properties that are not ordinarily considered part of its meaning or associated implications. This kind of process, by which the topic comes to be reconceptualized through the filter of the vehicle, is very different from a comparison in which each term retains its independent identity.

Because the relation between topic and vehicle is said to be *interactive,* the relationship cannot be entirely unidirectional: while the filter of the vehicle alters the identity of the topic, the topic also influences the nature of the filter. Consider the difference between calling the world an unweeded garden and likening someone's face to an unweeded garden. In the former case abstract properties of disorder, lack of control, and the domination of nature over reason come to the fore; in the latter physical properties such as lack of symmetry, messiness, and beardedness become prominent. Hence, the nature of the topic determines which of the vehicle's associated implications can be applied to the topic.

The advantage of the interaction view is twofold: (1) no assumption is made that a metaphor is reducible to its literal paraphrase, no matter how detailed the paraphrase; and (2) this view is consistent with the intuition that the similarity on which a metaphor is ultimately grounded is an asymmetrical one (Ortony et al., 1985).

• *Semantic versus Pragmatic Approaches to Metaphor*

Metaphors have been conceptualized either as special types of sentences or as special ways of using sentences that in other contexts could be nonmetaphoric. Semantic approaches to the problem of metaphor definition attempt to locate metaphoricity in the sentence itself, regardless of the context in which it is used (Cohen, 1979). In contrast, pragmatic approaches locate metaphoricity outside the sentence—in the speaker's *use* of the sentence, and hence in the speaker's *intentions* (Rumelhart, 1979; Saddock, 1979; Searle, 1979b). Whereas semantic accounts of metaphor attempt to distinguish metaphoric and literal sentences, pragmatic accounts attempt to distinguish metaphoric and literal uses of sentences.

Semantic theorists have relied for their examples on metaphors that are semantically anomalous or literally false. Standard examples include "Juliet is the sun," and "Dictionaries are gold-mines" (Ortony, 1979a); "The prison guard was a hard rock that could not be moved" (Winner, Rosenstiel, and Gardner, 1976); "Hair is spaghetti" (Billow, 1975); "Billy was a squirrel burying the nuts" (Vosniadou et al., 1984); "The car died" (Keil, 1979); "loud tie" (Winner and Gardner, 1977); and "He is a lion in battle" (Cohen, 1979). It is tempting to adopt a semantic approach to metaphor when considering such examples, all of which are distinguishable from literal sentences by their semantic structure. They are recognizably metaphoric because of their literal falsehood (hair is *not* spaghetti) and their violations of semantic selection restrictions (Katz and Fodor,

1963). For example, to apply "die" to an inanimate object, as in "The car died," is to violate the restriction that only animate things can be said to die.

The problem with the semantic approach is that many metaphoric utterances are neither literally false nor semantically anomalous. Out of context there is no way to know they are metaphoric. Hamlet's utterance, " 'Tis an unweeded garden" qualifies as such a case. It is metaphoric *only* in its context, when Hamlet is so clearly talking about human behavior. Transfer this sentence to the context of an actual garden and the sentence becomes literal. For metaphors such as this one no logical or grammatical analysis of the sentence in isolation will reveal that it is metaphorically (or, for that matter, literally) intended (Searle, 1979b). Thus, instead of distinguishing between metaphoric and literal sentences, we are better off making a distinction between metaphoric and literal *uses* of language and determining metaphoric use by the juxtaposition of a sentence in a particular context. As we will see, ironic utterances are also distinguishable from literal ones in terms of use but not grammatical structure.

According to the pragmatic approach to metaphor identification, the only necessary criterion for metaphor is that there be a sharp disjunction between sentence meaning and speaker meaning: the speaker must mean something jarringly different from what he says; and what he says he must not mean (Searle, 1979b). This disjunction is particularly important for metaphors that are not false or anomalous, because it is then the *only* property that distinguishes such metaphors from literal statements.

The Study of Irony

Irony is an omnipresent principle of language, found in even the most ordinary conversations. Recognizing the centrality of irony to language, the literary critic Kenneth Burke is cited by Booth (1974) as saying, "We cannot use language maturely until we are spontaneously at home in irony."

Verbal irony can occur at the level of the individual sentence, or it may pervade an entire text. In this way it is no different from metaphor. A sentence can contain one or two words used metaphorically; the entire sentence can be intended metaphorically; or a long passage can be intended metaphorically, as in allegory. Swift's *Gulliver's Travels* is one long extended metaphor (hence generally called an allegory), in which the various imaginary countries visited stand for aspects of England. Similarly, irony may reside at the word or sentence level, or may extend throughout an entire text, as in Swift's "Modest Proposal," in which the author takes an outrageous position—that children of the poor in Ireland be killed and eaten so as to avoid becoming an economic burden to their parents and country—in order to mock those politicians who showed too little concern for the poor of Ireland.

The clues alerting the listener that something is ironic are determined to some extent by whether the irony is sentential or textual. In sententially ironic statements, the contrast with the surrounding verbal context may provide a potent clue. In a text that is ironic throughout, the clues must be either the sheer outrageousness of the author's position (as in Swift's "Modest Proposal"), or the conflict between what is said and what we know about the speaker's beliefs (as in Hamlet's exclamation "Thrift, thrift").

As with any form of figurative language, irony consists in saying one thing but meaning another. In irony, however, the relationship between what is said and what is meant must entail some form of contradiction, incongruity, or incompatibility between evaluative propositions. Thus, an understanding of irony requires that one recognize the evaluative incongruity between what is said and what the speaker believes to be true.

It is too simple to say that in irony what is meant is simply the direct opposite of what is said. Although this formulation applies to conventional forms of irony, such as "You're a big help" (meaning "you're no help"), it is not sufficient for more complex novel forms (Kaufer, 1981). Hamlet does not mean to say that the motive for the hasty remarriage is lack of thrift.

Rather, he means that the marriage is explained by base motives and that those involved are so unfeeling they might even be imagined to place thrift above respect for the dead. Moreover, some ironic utterances are not propositions with truth value and hence have no clear opposites, as, for example, "Thanks loads." Nonetheless, some sense of opposition remains at the heart of irony. One espouses gratitude when ingratitude is deserved; one ascribes a positive motive (thrift) when a baser one is implied. The opposition in irony is not between the sentence meaning and its opposite, but rather between the speaker's attitude and the attitude implied by the literal meaning of the sentence. When one recognizes this opposition, one realizes that the speaker is not committed to his utterance (Kaufer, 1981).

The opposition between what is said and what is meant cannot be between *any* attitudes. It must involve a contradiction between praise and blame, between a positive and a negative evaluation. In the most common form of irony what is said is positive, but what is meant is negative. Hamlet's is one such example, as is "I see you got your usual high score," when the addressee has, as usual, just received a failing grade. But irony can also entail saying something negative to mean something positive (Cutler, 1974): "I see you got your usual low score," when the addressee has, as usual, received a high test score. Whenever a negative remark is intended ironically, however, it conveys overtones of negative as well as positive meaning (Cutler, 1974; Grice, 1978). The speaker who calls a high score "low" is making a left-handed compliment and is at best displaying an ambivalent attitude toward his rival's consistent success. The addressee is left without any easy response: although it is appropriate to act injured when one's low score is mocked as "high," it is not quite correct to act flattered when one's high score is mocked as "low."

There are ironic utterances that on the surface are neither negative nor positive in tone. For example, a mother may tell her son to be sure to put on his sweater. If the child comes downstairs without his sweater, the mother might say, "I see you are wearing your sweater." Although this utterance seems on the surface to be neutral in evaluative content, it does in fact convey a negative meaning. The opposition here is not only between wearing and not wearing a sweater (which in itself is not an opposition between positive and negative judgments), but also between obedient (positive) and forgetful (negative) behavior.

• Forms of Irony

As with metaphor, irony can take a number of different forms. An ironic utterance may be literally false, as in Hamlet's assertion (thrift was not the motive for the marriage). An ironic utterance may also be literally true, as in the example given earlier (in reply to "How was your blind date?" the answer "He had nice shoes"). An ironic utterance may be in the form of a rhetorical question and hence have no truth value ("When are you going to give your first performance at Carnegie Hall?" asked of an untalented violinist). An ironic utterance may be ambiguous so that its truth value is difficult to determine ("She is as smart as she is kind"). And irony may occur in a nonverbal form, as when one claps after someone blunders.

What all these forms of irony share is some kind of flouting of the maxims that ordinarily govern conversations (Grice, 1975). We ordinarily say what we believe to be true and relevant; we say as much as is necessary and no more, and we strive for clarity. The maxim of truth is violated by literally false irony; the maxim of relevance, by literally true irony; and the maxim of clarity, by ambiguous irony. Irony in the form of a rhetorical question to which the speaker already knows the answer does not seem to violate any Gricean maxim, but it causes the addressee difficulty in replying. Hence, such utterances violate the principle of properly maintaining a conversation.

• Victims of Irony

Irony conveys a negative, mocking attitude that is usually directed at someone in particular. The object of the ironist's attack is often called the *victim* of the irony. The speaker may mock himself, his addressee, an onlooker, or a person (or type of person) who is not present. Not all ironic utterances have victims: sometimes the speaker is simply expressing irritation at a situation for which there is no one to blame. In this case the victim is simply fate.

The victim of an ironic remark may or may not perceive the speaker's ironic intent. If the victim fails to perceive the irony, he becomes a victim in a second sense as well—by virtue of being too obtuse to understand the irony. When there is such a naive victim, there is usually a double audience: there is the naive victim who misses the point, and there is the party who not only gets the point but also laughs silently with the speaker at the naive victim's lack of understanding (Fowler, 1965).

Irony thus can be used to polarize an audience into initiates and noninitiates. The ironist conveys one meaning to the uninitiated and another to the initiated. Hence, the ironist solidifies his relationship with those who agree with his indirect meaning and distances himself from those who agree with his literal meaning (Kaufer, 1981). For instance, one might say, "There's nothing wrong with spending money on defense and cutting back on programs to help the poor" in the presence of two people, one of whom is a fiscal conservative and one of whom is a New Deal Democrat. The speaker intends the liberal (whose political views he shares) to recognize his utterance as ironic; but he intends the conservative (who will agree with the literal meaning of his remarks) to take him literally. In this situation there is a double audience. Moreover, the victim of the irony is a victim in two ways: he is first of all the object of the speaker's attack (the speaker is ridiculing those who hold the position espoused); and he is also the victim in the eyes of the speaker and the confederate by virtue of missing the point.

The naive victim need not even be the object of the speaker's mockery. In Swift's "Modest Proposal," for instance, readers at first take Swift's arguments literally and are horrified; at some later point (depending on the sophistication of the reader), the irony is detected and the reader moves from being the naive victim to being in collusion with the author against those who are really under attack—the Irish who collaborate with the English ruling classes on barbarous policies that ignore the plight of the poor.

What is ordinarily referred to as sarcasm is simply one form of irony. Irony is sarcastic if it is bitter and if its victim is an actual person rather than just an imagined *type* of person. Irony which mocks fate (as in "Isn't life easy?" said just when troubles are piling up), or which mocks oneself ("Great move," said by someone who has just dropped a tray of dishes) is not appropriately called sarcasm.

Whereas irony almost always has a victim (in one or both of the senses discussed above), metaphor rarely has a victim. This is because metaphor is not usually an attack on some position (although it can be used in this way) and also because it does not postulate a double audience, since it is too implausible to imagine a person so naive as to take a metaphor literally.

· *Theories of Irony*

Irony has traditionally been considered a form of meaning substitution in which the speaker says one thing to imply something contradictory. Hence, the hearer's task is to recognize that the speaker does not mean what he says and to substitute what is meant for what is said. Definitions of this kind follow from the "meaning substitution" theory of irony, which is as problematic as the equivalent view of metaphor. It does not tell us what motivates the substitution. If irony is but a stand-in for a literal utterance, then why bother to use it at all?

Recently, there have been two attempts to go beyond meaning substitution theories. Clark and Gerrig (1984) have argued for a "pretense" theory, which has its roots in classical accounts of irony (namely, Aristotle's); and Sperber (1984) has developed a "mention" theory of irony. Both of these newer theories have been offered to replace the meaning substitution approach (see Sperber, 1984). In my view, however, pretense and mention theories add to but do not replace a meaning substitution account.

According to the pretense theory, an ironic utterance does

not have two levels of meaning (the one said and the one meant). Rather, the ironic speaker is pretending to mean what he says, and there is no other level of meaning we are supposed to substitute. The speaker is pretending to be an injudicious person speaking to an unitiated audience. In other words, he pretends to be the kind of person who would literally intend such an utterance, in order to mock such a person, and also in order to mock those who would take him literally. On this account Hamlet is role-playing. He is pretending to be the kind of person who would think it a good thing to have the marriage so soon after the funeral so that the same foods could be used. In so doing he mocks the type of person who cannot see what is really going on—the lack of respect and lack of proper mourning for the dead king. The ingredient of opposition still remains, however. Instead of opposition between what he says and what he means (the substitution view), here the opposition inheres between what he really believes and what he pretends to believe.

Those who espouse the mention theory also reject the assumption that there are two levels of meaning, asserting that the only meaning is the literal one. The speaker does not *use* his utterance to convey meaning, as is ordinarily the case in language. Rather, the speaker *mentions* an utterance or thought previously spoken or held by someone, or attributable to certain types of people, and simultaneously—by various means such as tone of voice, context, and so on—conveys his negative *attitude* toward those who would say or believe such a thing. What is mentioned can be a thought that was verbally expressed, or a thought that has never been verbalized but is a received opinion. Thus, when Hamlet says, "Thrift, thrift," he echoes the kind of statement one would expect from someone who is morally blind. The opposition in mention theory is between what the speaker mentions (or those who would believe what the speaker mentions) and what the speaker believes.

In my view some uses of irony are best described as pretense, while others are best described as mention. To the extent that the speaker hopes to "dupe" the listener, if only momentarily, in order to shock him later with the recognition of irony, the speaker is pretending. In this case the speaker must make at least some half-hearted attempts at deceiving his audience: he may say something that is not prima facie implausible (in the midst of a rainstorm, for instance, the person who says, "I love this weather," could conceivably like rain) and he may adopt a sincere tone of voice or facial expression. To the extent that the speaker sends out clear signals that he does not agree with what he is saying, he may be more aptly described as mentioning a view while rejecting it. This occurs when the speaker adopts a sarcastic tone of voice, or when the utterance is blatantly false or out of character (as Hamlet's).

Neither mention nor pretense theory is incompatible with a meaning substitution view. If a speaker is pretending to mean what he says, then he does this not only to mock uninitiates but also to convey his real beliefs to an initiated audience. And his real beliefs can be considered to be part of his meaning. The listener must substitute the speaker's actual beliefs for those beliefs he professes to hold. Although philosophers of language may quarrel about where utterance meaning ends and speaker belief begins, this distinction makes little psychological difference. Clearly, part of the task of irony comprehension is to identify the speaker's actual beliefs. If a speaker is mentioning an utterance as he rejects it, he does this not only to mock those who believe such a view but also to convey his belief that this view is false. Again, his conveyed beliefs can be considered part of his message.

What pretense and mention theory add to meaning substitution views is an account that links irony closely to attitude or belief. Understanding irony involves more than a substitution of one proposition for another. Since irony carries with it evocations of the speaker's attitudes, its comprehension involves the unmasking of the speaker's beliefs. For instance, when in "A Modest Proposal" Swift calls for the cannibalism of children as a solution to the plight of the poor, we are not meant to substitute the opposite proposition—that cannibalism should be rejected. Were we to take this as his meaning, we would have missed the point. The import of Swift's essay is not that cannibalism is bad (no one doubts this), but that some elements of society act as barbarously as cannibals: by ignoring the poor, they are killing the poor. Swift is conveying his attitude toward society, and he is telling us whom he condemns and with whom he sides.

Thus, understanding irony involves substituting one meaning for another, although the meaning that is substituted is not simply the opposite of what is said. If irony were no more than this, one could not claim that irony is primarily a means of conveying attitudes. The meaning that is substituted in irony includes the speaker's beliefs about his utterance as well as his attitudes toward those who would espouse such a view. Irony is always in some general sense a form of meaning substitution, as is metaphor, since they are both indirect ways of conveying a message; pretense and mention are the two mechanisms by which the ironist can convey an implied meaning other than what follows directly from the surface statement. And the implied meaning that is conveyed through either pretense or mention is inextricably bound up with the speaker's *attitude* toward his topic of conversation.

The positions espoused here on metaphor and irony have implications for questions about the development of the abilities to understand these forms of language. With respect to metaphors, I have argued that although they can be semantically deviant, they are often quite ordinary sentences used in special ways. Hence, for children to understand metaphors, sensitivity to context is necessary: the hearer must use the context to interpret the speaker's meaning. I have also asserted that metaphor comprehension is an asymmetrically interactive process by which we come to see the topic as the vehicle, and in which the topic influences which aspects of the vehicle we apply to the topic. Any investigation of children's understanding of metaphor must address the question of whether children are sensitive to the asymmetrical topic-vehicle structure of metaphor.

With respect to irony, I have argued that the opposition at the heart of irony is conveyed either by pretense or by mention and that the task of the listener is to infer the implied, unstated meaning. Irony functions not to reconceptualize our world but rather to let us peer into the speaker's subjective world. Crucial to understanding irony is the ability to infer the speaker's actual beliefs and communicative intentions. The developmental issue thus becomes one of children's abilities to infer the contents of another's mind. And once children are able to recognize and understand irony, we must still ask whether they are sensitive to the advantages of using irony rather than a literal "equivalent." That is, we must ask whether they recognize the social effects of using irony rather than a literal paraphrase.

· Chapter 3 ·

Measures of Metaphor

As a young research assistant to Théodore Simon in Paris, Piaget was given the job of standardizing Burt's Test of Reasoning for young children. Included in this test was a section on proverbs. Fascinated by the systematic kinds of misunderstanding that children showed, Piaget later carried out his own study of children's understanding of proverbs. Piaget gave children aged nine, ten, and eleven a list of ten proverbs such as "Drunken once will get drunk again," "Little streams make mighty rivers," and "When the cat's away, the mice will play." These sayings were presented along with twelve sentences, in random order, ten of which expressed in different form the ideas captured by the proverbs. The child was given the task of reading the proverbs and finding their appropriate matches. For instance, the match for "Drunken once will get drunk again" was "It is difficult to break old habits."

The test results led Piaget to a strong conclusion. Most of the time, he found, the children "did not understand the proverbs in the least" (1974, p. 142). Oddly, however, the children were not aware of their misunderstanding and usually felt that they had fully understood the proverbs. Imagining that they had understood the proverbs, the children readily found a sentence which in their minds was a perfect match for the proverb.

Mat, aged ten, matched the proverb "So often goes the jug to water, that in the end it breaks" with the sentence "As we grow older we grow better," explaining that the proverb meant "You go to the water so often that the jug cracks; you go back once again and it breaks." He went on to state his understanding of the matching sentence: "The older you get the better you get and the more obedient you become." Pressed to explain how these two sentences mean the same thing, he replied, "Because the jug is not so hard because it is getting old, because the bigger you grow, the better you are and you grow old" (p. 150). This example demonstrates what Piaget calls the "illusion of understanding." Mat shows no uncertainty about the meaning of the proverb, despite the fact that to an adult his interpretation makes no sense. He also demonstrates what Piaget calls "syncretism" of reasoning, in which various elements (in this case, the two sentences) are fused idiosyncratically.

Evidence for Metaphor Comprehension as a Late Development

Since proverbs are based on the same kind of similarity as are metaphors, Piaget's study of proverbs suggests that the ability to understand metaphor is one of the last facets of language to develop, one which might even require the structures of formal operations (Inhelder and Piaget, 1958). This position was shared by Elkind (1969, 1974, 1976) and Pollio and Pollio (1974), who argued that understanding metaphor requires sophisticated metalinguistic skills that do not develop until late childhood. Studies of children's understanding of metaphor carried out in the 1960s and 1970s appear to confirm that metaphor comprehension is a skill that does not emerge until middle or late childhood (that is, after age eight or nine).

These studies support the hypothesis, outlined in Chapter 1, that for children the major stumbling block to understanding is the task of inferring what is meant (step 3). These studies show that children are able to recognize metaphors as nonliterally intended (the task of step 1) and to infer a meaning based on similarity (the task of step 2), but that they infer the *wrong kind of similarity*. What children most often do is find a sensory similarity between topic and vehicle when a nonsensory, relational similarity is at issue.

To see this distinction, it is helpful to return to the interaction view of metaphor, according to which the task of constructing a ground requires a transfer of salient properties from vehicle to topic, with the properties transferred being guided by the nature of the topic. In understanding a metaphor such as "The world is an unweeded garden," the only salient properties of gardens that are applicable to "world" are relational (nonphysical, functional) properties: unweeded gardens are disorganized, unruly, and chaotic. Nonrelational, physical properties such as having soil, plants, grass, and actual weeds are irrelevant to the metaphor and hence not transferable. Listeners must use the topic to filter out properties of the vehicle that are highly salient to the vehicle but that are clearly inapplicable to the topic.

In most metaphors physical properties yield in importance to relational ones (Carbonell, 1982; Gentner, 1983). We tend to ignore the physical attributes of a vehicle in favor of the relations in which it participates. We then map the relational structure of the vehicle term onto the topic term (Gentner, 1983). For instance, we map the relational properties of unweeded gardens, such as disordered and out of control, onto the world, ignoring such physical attributes of gardens as green, containing soil, and so on.

The importance of relational attributes in metaphoric similarity should not obscure the fact that metaphors may also be based primarily or exclusively on sensory attributes. Metaphors used in the service of physical description are prime examples. Take the following description, which I came across in John K. Fairbank's autobiography, *Chinabound* (1982). Looking out of an airplane, Fairbank saw "a solitary peak with a dusty landing strip being bulldozed all across the top of it." What flashed through his mind was an image of a "dentist working on a molar before he capped it" (p. 188). Although this is phrased not in the form of a metaphor, but as a literal description of his thought processes, it could serve as the conceptual underpinning of a verbal metaphor: the similarity between the landing strip and the molar is a metaphoric one, and it is based primarily on physical properties.

Perhaps the most clear-cut cases of metaphoric similarity based entirely on relational attributes are those explanatory analogies found in science: for example, the brain as a computer, the atom as a solar system, and the heart as a pump. In literary metaphors physical attributes always seem to retain some importance, even when the metaphors are based primarily on relational properties. For instance, "Juliet is the sun" not only means that Juliet is in the center of Romeo's universe, above him, bringing him hope (relational properties), but also perhaps hints that Juliet is warm, glowing, and shining (physical properties). Evidence that physical attributes are more likely to be involved in literary metaphors than in scientific analogies is provided by a study (Gentner, 1982) in which people rated these figures in terms of clarity (the precision of mapping between topic and vehicle) and richness (the sheer quantity of properties mapped). Good scientific analogies were rated as high in clarity, bad ones as high in richness. In contrast, good metaphors were not differentiated from bad ones by clarity ratings but were rated as richer than bad metaphors. If richer mappings tend to include physical properties (which, although not proven by this study, seems likely), we can conclude that physical properties of the vehicle are more likely to be transferred when given a literary metaphor than a scientific analogy.

The problem becomes, then, how we know when to map a vehicle's physical attributes onto the topic and when to map a vehicle's functional relations (Carbonell, 1982; Gentner, 1983). According to one solution, proposed by Carbonell (1982), we may assume that the mapping is relational unless we only know about physical properties of the vehicle. Hearing "John is a fox," for instance, we assume that John is sly, because we know this to be true of foxes. The fact that foxes are reddish in color is irrelevant, supplanted in importance by the behavioral information. But hearing "John is a giraffe," we conceive of John as very tall, because we know little about nonphysical aspects of giraffes. Hence, physical attributes might be mapped only by default, when we do not know what else to do.

There are cases, however, in which we know both types of information about the vehicle, and yet we map the physical attributes. A good example of this is the aforementioned description of a bulldozed landing strip as a molar smoothed by a dentist. Clearly we possess a great deal of knowledge about the function as well as the appearance of teeth. But in this case we know that it is the appearance of teeth that is at issue, and we know this from the context of the topic in question—the sight of a landing strip from above. Adults seem to know when to transfer physical properties and when to transfer relational ones. But children appear to have difficulty with this. As mentioned above, they tend to transfer physical properties when they should be transferring relational ones. This proclivity has been demonstrated in numerous studies.

In one of the first studies of children's metaphor comprehension, Asch and Nerlove (1960) interviewed children between the ages of three and twelve about the meaning of *dual-function* adjectives. These adjectives are terms such as "hard," "warm," and "sweet," terms that refer to a physical property but that can be metaphorically extended to the psychological domain (a *hard* person, a *warm*-hearted friend, a *sweet* disposition). To understand such usage, one must be able to perceive nonsensory connections between physical properties and psychological states.

Asch and Nerlove first ascertained that children understood the literal, physical reference of these terms by placing in front of them a series of objects and asking them to point to objects with specific physical properties: the cold one (ice water), the sweet one (a sugar cube), the soft one (a powder puff), and so on. Next, the children were questioned to determine whether they understood the metaphoric (psychological) meaning of these terms. For each term, they were asked questions such as: "Are people cold? Do you know any cold people? How do you know they are cold? What do they do or say when they are cold?"

Preschoolers had no difficulty understanding the physical reference of these terms, correctly pointing to the cold, sweet, and soft objects. But they demonstrated no understanding of the psychological reference of these terms, denying that people could be cold, sweet, and soft. In contrast, five- and six-year-olds were willing to apply these terms to people, but *only* in the physical sense of the term. Hence, cold people were people who were not warmly dressed; hard people had firm muscles. Not until between the ages of seven and ten were children able to understand the psychological meaning of such terms. And only eleven- and twelve-year-olds could articulate the link between the physical and psychological senses of the terms, explaining, for instance, that "hard things and hard people are both unmanageable." Asch and Nerlove's findings, which were confirmed and extended by Lesser and Drouin (1975), suggest that metaphor comprehension is not fully developed until preadolescence. This claim is a controversial one that is supported by some studies but refuted by others, at least in its strong form.

In more recent studies children were asked to discover the ground in copula metaphors. Winner, Rosenstiel, and Gardner (1976) constructed two types of metaphorical sentences containing dual-function adjectives: psychological-physical ones, such as those used by Asch and Nerlove ("After many years of working at the jail, the prison guard had become a hard rock that could not be moved"); and cross-sensory ones, linking colors and sounds, smells and sounds, smells and brightness, and so on ("The smell of her perfume was bright sunshine"). Children were asked to explain the meaning of the metaphors.

Six-year-olds were unable to offer any interpretation in 25% of the responses. When able to do so, they divided their responses among three kinds: literal, metonymic, and primitive-metaphoric. Most frequent were interpretations classified as "metonymic" and "primitive-metaphoric" (26% and 27%, respectively). In metonymic responses no similarity was noted between topic and vehicle. Rather, the two terms were woven into an associative relationship. For example, the prison guard metaphor was paraphrased as "The guard worked in a prison with hard rock walls"; and the perfume metaphor was paraphrased as "When she was standing outside in the sun she was wearing perfume." These interpretations are grounded in an *association* rather than a *similarity* between the topic and vehicle: hence, they reflect a failure at step 2.

In the primitive-metaphoric interpretations children based their interpretations on a similarity between topic and vehicle—hence they succeeded at step 2—but the similarity noted was a sensory one, hence failure at step 3. Children applied the dual-function adjective in its primary sense to both topic and vehicle. To call a prison guard a hard rock meant that he had hard, tough muscles: here, "hard" retains its physical sense, and the guard and the rock are both hard in the same sense. To call perfume bright sunshine meant that it was bright yellow in color: here "bright" retains its visual sense. Such interpretations were considered *primitive* (not fully developed) because they were based on a transfer of physical properties in cases where relational properties should have been transferred.

Less frequently, six-year-olds offered literal responses in which the entire sentence was taken literally: "The king had a magic rock and he turned the guard into another rock"; "Her perfume was made out of rays from the sun." In literal interpretations children projected features from the vehicle onto the topic that did not conform to the topic: they altered the topic so that it shared features with the vehicle that in fact the topic did not possess. Such literal interpretations were often given a fairy-tale explanation in order to render them plausible. This kind of interpretation was considered the least appropriate of all, and was given in only 12% of the responses from six-year-olds; literal interpretations occurred with considerably less frequency at all older ages.

At eight years of age, children continued to offer primitive-metaphoric interpretations (33%) but offered many fewer metonymic ones (12%). In striking contrast to the younger children's responses, 30% of the responses from eight-year-olds could be coded as "genuine-metaphoric." The guard was now seen as "mean," someone who "did not care about the feelings of the prisoners." And the perfume metaphor was understood to be a reference to the perfume's pleasant smell. By ten years of age, children gave genuine-metaphoric interpretations in 48% of their responses, and metonymic and primitive-metaphoric interpretations less often than at previous ages.

Just at the age when children began to offer genuine-metaphoric interpretations—at eight and ten years—they also began to offer interpretations that were almost, but not quite, right. For instance, the guard was taken to be "fussy"—a psychological trait, and an appropriately negative one, but the *wrong* trait. And the perfume was understood as "fancy"—a nonvisual trait, but once again, the wrong trait. These responses were coded as "inappropriate-metaphoric": they are close to genuine-metaphoric interpretations in that the dual-function term is modified when it is applied to the topic. The guard is no longer seen as physically similar to the rock; and the perfume no longer as visually similar to sunshine. Instead, the child has come up with a more relational kind of similarity linking topic and vehicle.

Although the precise similarity was often not grasped, it is noteworthy that the polarity of the mapping was usually correct in some respects. For instance, children sensed that to call a person a hard rock was to say something negative: hence the guard was seen as fussy (a negative trait) and never as kind or funny (positive traits). In the primitive-metaphoric interpretations the similarity discovered was genuine but the match was made to the wrong kinds of properties (sensory ones). In the inappropriate-metaphoric interpretations the "similarity" discovered was not genuine similarity (physically hard and psychologically fussy do not quite match) but the match was made to the appropriate kinds of properties (psychological ones).

We can conclude from this study that when children are given context-free metaphors that bridge elements from the physical and psychological domains or elements from two sensory modalities, they generate interpretations which can be hierarchically ordered, and full comprehension is not apparent until age ten. Least sophisticated (and occurring primarily among the youngest children) are literal and metonymic interpretations; next in appropriateness and sophistication are primitive-metaphoric interpretations (which occur with most frequency among eight-year-olds); next come inappropriate-metaphoric interpretations (which occur primarily among ten-year-olds); and finally, genuine-metaphoric interpretations (which occur with increasing frequency from the age of ten onward).

Very similar results were obtained in a later study by Johnson (1982). Again, children were asked to generate their own interpretations for metaphors presented free of prior context. In this case no dual-function adjectives were used to bridge the topic and vehicle: hence the metaphors were more open to alternative interpretations. Sample metaphors included "My sister was a rock," "My sister was a butterfly," and "My shirt was a rock." Johnson demonstrated four developmental levels of interpretations, which she labeled "projection," "identity," "analogy," and "predicate" mappings. As we will see, Johnson's levels correspond to the types of responses in the study by Winner and colleagues (discussed above): projection mappings correspond to literal responses, identity mappings to primitive-metaphoric responses, and analogy and predicate mappings to genuine-metaphoric responses.

The two most frequent types of interpretation given by Johnson's six-year-old subjects were literal (projection) and primitive-metaphoric (identity). Examples of literal responses included "Like your shirt was exactly the same as a rock" in response to "My shirt was a rock," and "My sister could fly like one and she's got antennas like one and wings like one" in response to "My sister was a butterfly."

An example of a primitive-metaphoric interpretation of "My sister was a rock" was "She was hard, like if you felt her hand you couldn't squish it or anything." Just as the prison guard was seen in Winner and associates' 1976 study as physically hard, here the sister is seen as hard in the same way as a rock. Another child at this age interpreted this metaphor to mean

"She just sat there and didn't move." Here the sister is physically immovable in the same way as a rock. And in response to "My sister is a butterfly," one child reasoned that "She might have pants or a shirt as colorful as wings." Such interpretations occurred in about a third of the responses from six-year-olds, confirming the findings of the 1976 study.

Eight-year-olds rarely offered literal interpretations but continued to offer primitive-metaphoric ones at the same frequency as reported in Winner, Rosenstiel, and Gardner (1976)—in about one third of their responses. Children at this age also began to offer "analogical" interpretations (in about a fifth of the responses). Analogical responses are a form of genuine-metaphoric interpretation in which a relational property is applied to the topic. For example, the sister was seen not as physically hard but rather as "unyielding."

Ten-year-olds offered analogical interpretations in a third of their responses and also began to offer predicate interpretations (15%). Predicate interpretations are analogical ones taken one step further: after applying a feature from vehicle to topic, subjects giving this type of response went on to elaborate the features of the topic so that it was described in terms no longer applicable to the vehicle. For example, given "My sister is a rock," one child said this meant she was "mean." (At the analogical level, this child would have said the sister was hard in the sense of unyielding—supplying a generic term that applied to both psychological and physical hardness). In contrast, at the predicate level children elaborated "psychologically hard" and came up with "mean"—a term that can in no way apply to a rock. Such a response represents a further accommodation of vehicle features to the topic. Other examples include "It's starchy" for "My shirt was a rock"; "She's a twin" for "My sister was a mirror"; and "She's shy" for "My sister was a butterfly."

For twelve-year-olds, predicate mappings began to replace analogical mappings: predicate mappings were offered in about a third of the responses from children this age. Adults offered twice as many predicate mappings as analogical ones. The frequency of primitive-metaphoric responses declined steadily with age, after age eight.

Johnson's findings once again suggest that the ability to generate interpretations for metaphors is a late development: literal and primitive-metaphoric interpretations give way to analogical ones, and these in turn give way to further elaborations of analogical interpretations, the predicate mappings.

Factors Affecting Age of Metaphor Comprehension

• The Role of Context

Studies such as those reviewed above have been criticized because they require children to make sense of metaphors (or proverbs) presented out of context, whereas metaphors are ordinarily encountered in rich situational or verbal contexts. A person who shows psychological strength and loyalty is called a "rock"; but a person with well-developed muscles might also be so described. Similarly, a person wearing bright colors is described as a "butterfly," as is a person who flits from one activity to the next. Surely children must ordinarily make use of the context to make sense of metaphors: "butterfly" in reference to a colorfully dressed person will be understood differently from its reference to a restless person.

Thus, we cannot use the paraphrases of metaphors presented out of context to conclude that children cannot generate relational interpretations of metaphors when called for. If we are to learn how children understand metaphors as they ordinarily encounter them, then we must present metaphors in context. Tasks that present metaphors in context reveal the kinds of similarities that children *recognize* (Ortony, Reynolds, and Arter, 1978; Winner, Wapner, Cicone, and Gardner, 1979). Tasks that require interpretations generated with no context reveal the kinds of similarity that children *generate* on their own.

• The Difficulty of a Metalinguistic Response Measure

Studies showing late emergence of metaphor comprehension have also been criticized for their reliance on metalinguistic response measures (Vosniadou, 1987). The question of what response from the child should count as an index of comprehension has plagued research on metaphor. In the studies that have found late comprehension, understanding was assessed verbally by asking children to paraphrase metaphors—"What does it mean to say . . . ?" (Johnson, 1982; Winner, Rosenstiel, and Gardner, 1976). Others have asked children to select the appropriate verbal paraphrase, a multiple-choice measure (for example, Winner, Rosenstiel, and Gardner, 1976), or to judge whether sentences make sense or are anomalous (Shantiris, 1983). Comprehension has also been assessed nonverbally by asking children to point to the picture that best shows the metaphor's meaning—again, a multiple-choice measure (Honeck, Sowry, and Voegtle, 1976; Winner, Wapner, Cicone, and Gardner, 1979), to match words to visual stimuli on the basis of metaphoric similarity (Gardner, 1974; Marks and Hammeal, 1981; Winner, McCarthy, and Gardner, 1980), or to act out the metaphors using toy props (Vosniadou, Ortony, Reynolds, and Wilson, 1984). At the extreme, nonverbal measures may involve only nonverbal stimuli to match (Dent, 1984; Kogan et al., 1980; Lewkowicz and Turkewitz, 1980; Wagner et al., 1981): in such a paradigm matches made on the basis of metaphoric similarity, rather than on the basis of a literal resemblance or a random response, are used as a measure of metaphoric perception.

The measure used dramatically affects the level of comprehension revealed. The greater the reliance on linguistic and metalinguistic abilities, the more likely is the measure to reveal a low level of understanding. The measure which relies most heavily on linguistic and metalinguistic skills is paraphrase, and the argument for using this measure is that it will not overrepresent what the child understands. If the child gives an appropriate paraphrase, one can be certain that he has truly understood the metaphor. But paraphrase measures have the drawback of potentially underestimating the level of understanding, when given to young children. Undoubtedly, children understand metaphors before they can successfully explain their understanding.

A comparison of performance on paraphrase and multiple-choice measures reveals consistently higher performance when multiple-choice measures are used. For instance, Winner, Rosenstiel, and Gardner (1976) asked children not only to paraphrase metaphors but also to choose from four possible verbal paraphrases. Not surprisingly, children who failed on the paraphrase measure often succeeded on the multiple-choice measure. Pollio and Pickens (1980) also reported higher performance on a multiple-choice than a paraphrase measure. Multiple-choice tasks, however, are also not without drawbacks. They may either underrepresent or overrepresent level of understanding, depending entirely on the type and range of choices provided. When no literal or primitive-metaphoric choices are available, and the choices are restricted to those that are either correct or the polar opposite of the correct choice, preschoolers usually select the correct choice (Winner, Wapner, Cicone, and Gardner, 1979). In contrast, if correct choices must be distinguished from those that are partially correct or that paraphrase the metaphor literally, children are less likely to select the correct paraphrase.

To illustrate, in one study (Gardner, 1974) children were asked to match polar opposite terms (such as loud/quiet) to pairs of visual stimuli (such as thick lines/thin lines). Here, the only two possible choices were to match the term "loud" to thick lines or to thin lines, the latter being the direct opposite of the appropriate match. Successful performance on this task shows that children are sensitive to the overall polarity of terms such as "loud" (that is, that "loud" means "a lot of something").

Children as young as three and four years of age performed at a level above chance. It has since been determined that had children been given literal choices (such as a line with a mouth at the end, seen to be yelling), they might have performed less well. When Winner and Gardner (1978) provided literal as well as metaphoric pictorial choices for metaphoric sentences such as "That was a really loud tie," they found that six-year-olds were as likely to pick the literal as the appropriate picture.

A study by Vosniadou and Ortony (1986) clearly demonstrates the effect of response measure on outcome. Children were read stories ending with metaphoric sentences describing actions. One of the stories described a mother accompanying her shy child on the first day of school. The child (Sally) gets out of the car, looks at the school, and feels scared. The story ends with the metaphoric sentence, "Sally was a bird flying to her nest." Asked to paraphrase the sentence, six-year-olds often offered literal explanations; either they said that Sally had turned into a bird, or they ignored Sally and just talked literally about a bird. In contrast, when asked to enact the metaphor's meaning with dolls, children were more likely to demonstrate adequate understanding by taking the Sally figure and making her run to the mother doll.

Although this study shows that children may understand a metaphor without being able to paraphrase it, it is important to remember that even such a nonmetalinguistic task as Vosniadou's enactment measure is constrained by choices made in constructing the measure. For example, children were provided with toy human figures but not with toy birds and toy nests. Thus, there was no way that children could have enacted the metaphor literally. Had such literal props been available, children might have used them. Again we see that multiple-choice tasks can overestimate the child's understanding (by not providing literal choices) or underestimate understanding (by providing confusing choices). And this is true whether the multiple choice used is a verbal one (as in Winner et al., 1976) or a nonverbal one (as in Gardner, 1974; Vosniadou and Ortony, 1986; Winner and Gardner, 1977, 1978). In addition, the alternatives provided may be unrepresentative of the responses that children of different ages are likely to give. Thus, children may select an incorrect choice because it seems to be the best one available, even though they would not have come up with such a response on their own.

The lesson to be learned is that there is no "pure" measure of metaphor comprehension. There is no measure that reveals a child's level of understanding uncontaminated by the type of response the child must make to demonstrate understanding. It has been argued that studies which show metaphor to be a late ability are methodologically unsound because of their reliance on metalinguistic paraphrase measures and their lack of context (see Ortony, Reynolds, and Arter, 1978; Vosniadou et al., 1984). But I believe such studies are valuable because they reveal the ways in which children of different ages make sense of metaphors when the solution is suggested neither by the context nor by the alternative responses offered by the experimenter on a multiple-choice task. Comprehension as assessed verbally may be a very different and more sophisticated kind of skill than comprehension as assessed through nonverbal, perceptual, or enactive measures. And comprehension as revealed through open response measures may be a very different kind of ability from comprehension as revealed through multiple choice.

The issue here is of course not unique to metaphor. As with all psycholinguistic research, there is no pure measure of competence divorced from performance, and even grammaticality judgments may measure performance rather than competence. In memory research we distinguish between memory as assessed through recognition and recall, we distinguish between verbal and nonverbal tests of classification, and so on. Similarly, no conclusion about metaphor comprehension—its presence or its absence—is justified without the additonal clause "as assessed by a certain measure." However, because paraphrase measures can underestimate but not overestimate the child's understanding, we can feel confident that when a child is able to paraphrase a metaphor appropriately, he truly understands it. Moreover, this child should certainly succeed at any parallel multiple-choice task, whether verbal or nonverbal.

• *Knowing What Is Expected*

The child's faulty assessment of exactly what is being asked of him is another factor that may account for the persistence of step 3 errors through middle childhood. The task of explaining the meaning of a metaphoric sentence is hardly a task frequently encountered outside the psychological laboratory. The ability to reflect on sentences out of context is a skill that develops with age (Olson and Hildyard, 1980) and that affects metaphor comprehension when metaphors are presented out of context.

When asked to paraphrase a metaphor, the child must recognize that the experimenter probably knows the answer and is asking not out of a desire to understand the metaphor better but out of a desire to see what the child understands (see Perner, Leekam, and Wimmer, 1984, for a discussion of the problem with respect to conservation tasks). The child needs to know that he is expected to articulate fully his understanding, regardless of what he assumes the experimenter to know. Difficulty in recognizing this could result in insufficient paraphrases. For example, I have found that children are much more puzzled by a request to paraphrase a literal than a metaphoric utterance. It appears as if children take literal statements as well as easily understood metaphors for granted, and assume that no one would seriously question their understanding of sentences whose meanings are so clear. Hence, a scanty response to a request to paraphrase could indicate that the metaphor is so clear to the child that he cannot step back from it and explain it.

A second pragmatic concept the child must master is that language can be used to say something different from what is meant (Olson, 1977). This knowledge is necessary to allow success at step 1. Given a metaphor, the listener must recognize that the speaker means not that the topic really *is* the vehicle, but rather that the topic is *like* the vehicle in certain respects, or that the topic has certain of the vehicle's properties. The child must know the rules of the language game: that words can be used literally as well as nonliterally, and that one must recognize when a speaker is being nonliteral. The fact that children find similes easier to comprehend than metaphors (Reynolds and Ortony, 1980) suggests that children have difficulty understanding that it is permissible to say something that one does not mean. In a simile the relationship between the two terms is made explicit, and the child does not need to infer that the speaker really means that X is like Y. For the same reason children perform better when metaphors are rephrased in the form of riddles or analogies (Winner, Engel, and Gardner, 1980). In both of these cases the task is made explicit for the child and there is no need to infer an indirect meaning.

• *Information-Processing Demands*

The number of operations that must be performed on a metaphoric utterance in order to render it comprehensible may be yet another factor affecting the level of interpretation offered. Vosniadou and colleagues (1984) examined the role of two processing variables on comprehension: the predictability of the metaphor's meaning given its context, and the complexity of the metaphor as defined by the number of metaphoric terms and whether the similarity relationship was directly or indirectly stated.

Three related studies were carried out. In the first, children (in preschool, and first and third grades) heard brief stories each followed by a metaphoric utterance. The method used was the enactment paradigm described above. Half of the metaphoric utterances described highly predictable outcomes of the preceding context, while the other half described less predictable outcomes. For instance, in a story in which Billy sneaks some cookies and is about to be caught by his mother, the probable ending used was "Billy was a squirrel burying the nuts" (meaning that he hid the cookies). The improbable ending used was "Billy was a squirrel heading for his tree" (meaning that he ran to his room). Whether a story outcome was predictable or not was determined by a pilot study in which children had to enact what happened next, without the final sentence to guide them. In the pilot study, children were more likely to make Billy hide the cookies than to make him run to his room; hence, the metaphor of "burying the nuts" described a more likely outcome than that of "heading for his tree." In addition to metaphoric endings, there were also literal ones ("Billy was a child hiding the cookies/running to his room").

Children had no difficulty with the literal utterances, whether or not they were predictable from the story context. Children also had no difficulty with the metaphoric utterances, provided that these utterances described predictable outcomes: 85% of the preschoolers' answers were correct. When the metaphors described unpredictable outcomes, however, the number of correct responses dropped dramatically. For instance, for preschoolers, correct responses declined from 85% to 23%; and even for third graders, the figures were 93% and 68%.

One might argue that responses to the predictable metaphors had nothing at all to do with the metaphors and were simply due to guessing the most likely outcome given the preceding context. That this was not the case is shown by comparison with a control group who received only the contexts and no final utterances. Children in this group were less likely, for instance, to make Billy hide his cookies than were children who heard "Billy was a squirrel burying the nuts." Thus, it is clear that children were to some extent processing the predictable metaphors. In the case of the less predictable metaphors, however, preschoolers did no better than children in the control group, thus demonstrating that the presence of the metaphors had no effect on their responses.

This study underscores the importance of context in metaphor comprehension. It also shows that difficulty in understanding metaphor on the part of preschoolers is caused not by any inherent inability to understand metaphors (since preschoolers understood the predictable ones) and not by a problem with unpredictability per se (since preschoolers had no difficulty with the unpredictable literal utterances). Instead, the problem seems to lie in the increased information-processing demands caused by the *conjunction* between metaphoricity and unpredictability from context.

A second study by these researchers investigated the effect of increasing the number of metaphoric terms in the utterance to be understood. The sentences with more metaphoric terms also involved a new part of speech—a verb. In a sentence such as "Sally was a bird flying to her nest" (referring to a shy child running to her mother), three words are used metaphorically—"bird," "nest," and "flying." In contrast, in "Kenny and Andy were puppies following their master," only the two nouns ("puppies" and "master") are used metaphorically, whereas the verb ("following") can be interpreted literally. Children were asked to act out predictable and unpredictable metaphors, each with either two or three metaphoric terms.

When the task was to enact a sentence that had additional sources of difficulty (either the sentence was unpredictable or it contained three terms), the number of correct responses declined. When children were asked to act out the meanings of sentences involving three terms (two nouns and one verb), they performed much worse (only 28% of preschoolers' responses were correct, for example) than when two substitutions were involved (63% of their responses were correct). Sentences in which the verb must be taken metaphorically yielded more literal enactments (pretending that Billy was a squirrel burying nuts) and more partially literal enactments (pretending that Billy was a squirrel burying cookies). The most dramatic decline occurred when the task was to enact a sentence that was both unpredictable and that involved three metaphoric terms including a verb. This suggests that comprehension difficulty may well be due to the cumulative effects of these two sources of difficulty. But whether the difficulty of adding the third term was due to the greater number of terms, or to the use of a verb (which provides relational information), or to both, cannot be determined.

In a third study the cumulative effect of nonpredictability and presence of three metaphoric terms was examined using similes rather than metaphors. Metaphors in the form "X is Y" can be construed as indirect statements of the form "X is like Y." Hence, to interpret a metaphor in this form correctly, the listener must transform the nonexplicitly stated relationship "is a" to the explicitly stated relationship "is like a."

Again, preschoolers were found capable of handling two but not three levels of difficulty. They offered correct enactments for predictable similes with only two terms (level 1 in difficulty), and correct enactments for predictable similes with three terms (level 2) as well as unpredictable similes with two terms (level 2). Where they failed was in enacting the meanings of unpredictable similes with three terms (level 3). Moreover, a comparison of this and the second study showed that performance level at all degrees of difficulty was lower when the utterance was a metaphor than when it was a simile.

This series of studies allows the following conclusions. Difficulty in understanding metaphor cannot be attributed to any one factor alone. Rather, the sources of difficulty appear to have a cumulative and interactive effect. Preschool children may fail when the task involves more than one source of difficulty. Preschoolers can understand unpredictable metaphors better if they involve two metaphoric terms (or do not involve a verb as a metaphoric term) but can understand predictable metaphors even if they involve three metaphoric terms, including a verb. Six-year-olds can comprehend the predictable metaphors at all levels of difficulty but not the unpredictable metaphors beyond level 1. Thus, children of all ages tested here can understand less predictable metaphors, but only at the expense of one of the other variables. Something has to give. If we increase the difficulty of one factor (such as predictability), we must reduce the difficulty of another factor (such as number of terms) or performance level will decline. Hence, difficulty in understanding metaphor depends on the cumulative effects of various sources of difficulty, each of which requires that the listener perform some operation on the input.

Failure to Perceive the Asymmetry of Metaphors

We have seen that metaphor comprehension (including the ability to understand relational metaphors) is within the competence of the young child if the task is facilitated in one of several ways. But when children appear to comprehend a metaphor, they may remain insensitive to its asymmetry. If children show evidence of comprehension, yet at the same time remain oblivious to the asymmetry of a metaphor, they cannot be said to understand the metaphor in the same way as an adult does.

There is by now ample evidence that metaphors work asymmetrically and that the process of ground construction requires that salient properties of the vehicle be applied to the topic. As discussed in Chapter 2, the asymmetry of a metaphor is due to an imbalance in the salience of the properties shared by the topic and vehicle, such that the shared properties are more salient to the vehicle than the topic (Ortony, 1979a). Thus, in "Juliet is the sun," the properties shared by "Juliet" and "sun"—glowing, central, warm, life-giving, and so on—are more salient to "sun" than to "Juliet." Similarly, in "Billboards are warts on the highway" (from Ortony, 1979a), the shared property of "ugly protrusion" is more salient to warts than to billboards. The most salient property of billboards—that they are forms of advertisement—is not shared at all by warts.

If metaphors are asymmetrical in this way, the ground ought to be more highly related to the vehicle than to the topic, since the ground consists of properties more salient to the vehicle than to the topic (Ortony et al., 1985; see also Verbrugge and McCarrell, 1977). When subjects are given ground and either topic or vehicle and asked to rate the ground in terms of how applicable to, central to, or characteristic of the topic or vehicle it is, ratings are consistently higher for vehicles than for topics (Ortony et al., 1985). Thus, subjects ought to rate the properties of "glowing, central, warm, life-giving" as more characteristic of the sun than of Juliet. And if subjects heard "glowing, central, warm, life-giving," they should be more likely to infer the missing term of "Juliet is the ———" than to infer the missing term of "——— is the sun."

This salience imbalance, whereby shared properties are more highly related to the vehicle than to the topic, exists to some extent in literal similarity statements as well. Tversky (1977) noted that when we compare two elements which belong to the same category, we tend to let the first term of the comparison be the less prototypical member of the category. Hence, when we compare North Korea to China, we say "North Korea is like China" rather than "China is like North Korea." Although literal comparison statements are also characterized by salience imbalance, however, the salience imbalance in metaphors is much more extreme than that in literal similarity statements.

As discussed in Chapter 2, literal comparisons link elements that share attributes of high salience to both terms (Ortony, 1979a). It is for this reason that reversing a literal comparison (for example, "China is like North Korea") does not render the comparison nonsensical but only slightly alters its meaning. In contrast, reversing a metaphoric comparison radically alters the meaning. Sometimes a new meaning is created, as in "Some surgeons are butchers," as opposed to "Some butchers are surgeons." Most often, however, the reversal makes little sense ("The sun is Juliet"; "An unweeded garden is the world"; "A wart is a billboard").

Ortony (1979a) notes that adults are sensitive to the salience imbalance in metaphors. For example, when we hear the metaphor "Some surgeons are butchers," we take it to mean something negative about surgeons—that some of them are heavy-handed, imprecise, not to be trusted. But when the metaphor is reversed as "Some butchers are surgeons," we take this to mean something positive about butchers—that some are as skilled, careful, and precise as surgeons. The meaning of the metaphor is thus constrained by the order of its two terms. And people express strong and consistent preferences for similes in which the topic and vehicle are ordered in one way rather than another (Kogan et al., 1980; Ortony et al., 1985; Verbrugge, 1980). For instance, they prefer to hear "An education is like a stairway" than "A stairway is like an education" (Ortony et al., 1985). But people show much weaker preferences for order of terms in literal comparisons ("An escalator is like a stairway") or anomalous comparisons ("A polite manner is like an escalator"). Thus, the order of the terms in metaphoric similarity statements is highly constrained. Moreover, when metaphoric similarity statements (but not literal or anomalous ones) are reversed, the perceived similarity between topic and vehicle is sharply reduced. Interestingly, the perceived similarity of the terms in the preferred order for the similes is as high as that for literal comparisons (Ortony et al., 1985). For example, education is felt to be as similar to a stairway as a stairway is to an escalator. Thus, the similarities underlying metaphors are as strong as those underlying literal comparisons. Further support for the salience imbalance model comes from Hanson (1982), Harwood and Verbrugge (1977), and Katz (1982).

Only a few studies have examined children's sensitivity to asymmetry and salience imbalance in metaphor. Connor and Kogan (1980) used a task they had first tried with adults. When adults are given pairs of metaphorically related pictures or words and are asked to write sentences in the form "A is like B because . . . ," they often agree about the preferred order of terms. Connor and Kogan presented adults with forty pairs of terms. Of these, about half of the pairs yielded significant inter-subject agreement on the preferred order. Most of the asymmetrical pairs involved terms from different levels of an implicit conceptual hierarchy—humans, animals, plants, and objects—with the higher level term serving as the topic. Thus, given terms from the human and plant domains, subjects were more likely to place the human in the topic position.

When the same task was administered to high school students, significant intersubject agreement about order was found. Fifth and seventh graders, however, showed no such intersubject agreement (Connor and Martin, 1982), suggesting that children at this age are insensitive to asymmetry in metaphor.

To test whether this lack of sensitivity is part of a general lack of sensitivity found with literal similarity statements as well, Connor (1983) asked children in third, fifth, and seventh grades, as well as college students, to view pairs of slides and to write for each pair a sentence in the form "———— is like ————." The slides were either "literal comparison pairs" or "metaphoric comparison pairs." Literal pairs were taken from a task devised by Rosch (1975): each pair contained a highly typical instance of a category and a more peripheral instance (for example, red and pink; a vertical line and an oblique line; a car and a bicycle). Metaphoric comparison pairs contained pictures of objects from different categories: a tired, stooping old man and a gnarled tree; a woman with long curly hair and a plant with long curly vines. The metaphoric items were those administered to high school and college students by Connor and

Kogan (1980), in which high levels of agreement had been found with respect to order of terms.

Subjects' sentences were coded in terms of which pair member served as topic. Adults placed the most prototypical instance in the second place in 65% of their responses, yielding statements such as "Pink is like red," rather than "Red is like pink." The prototypical instances were the filters through which the less prototypical instances were viewed. Among seventh graders, almost 50% of the responses showed this pattern; among fifth graders, only 25% of the responses showed asymmetry. When the task was administered to third graders, no order preferences were found except for pairs of numbers.

On the basis of these studies, Connor and Kogan concluded that recognition of asymmetry in either literal or metaphoric similarity is not present in early childhood. But the measure of intersubject agreement may not be the most sensitive measure to use. Individual children may have idiosyncratic order preferences. Moreover, not having a preference does not mean that one cannot sense differences in meaning when order is reversed.

Using a less problematic measure, Cerbin (1985) also concluded that children are insensitive to the asymmetry of metaphors. In this study four-year-olds were asked to identify grounds of metaphors in the form "X is like Y" and "X and Y are alike." Cerbin called the first form a "directed comparison" and the second form a "nondirected comparison." In each type of comparison some of the pairs of terms shared a property of high salience to each term (for example, marshmallow and pillow: "softness" is salient to both); and some shared a property of high salience to one term and of low salience to the other term (boat and leaf: "floats" is more salient to boat than to leaf). The comparison statements were presented in one order to one group of subjects and in the other order to another group. There were three findings of interest.

First, children were more likely to identify the ground when it was a property of high salience to both terms than when it was of mixed salience. Thus, children were more likely to say that a marshmallow is like a pillow because it is soft than to say that a leaf is like a boat because it floats. Not surprisingly, nonsalient properties of objects were more difficult to call to mind than salient properties.

Second, children identified more mixed salience grounds in directed than in nondirected comparisons. This shows that they interpret the two linguistic forms differently. One possibility suggested by Cerbin is that children interpret a statement in the form "X and Y are alike because . . ." to mean that X and Y are practically the same. If children do not readily recognize how X and Y are the same, they may instead protest and reflect on how they differ. Consistent with this interpretation, children gave more such difference responses in the nondirected comparisons.

Finally, and most important for our purposes, the order of terms had no effect on the difficulty of ground identification for directed comparisons. Thus, an utterance in which the ground was of high salience to the vehicle ("a leaf is like a boat") was not found easier to interpret than an utterance in which the ground was of high salience to the topic ("a boat is like a leaf"). Children were as likely to say "floats" to "leaf" as to "boat."

Cerbin takes these findings to show that children are not interpreting metaphors according to the interactionist model of metaphor comprehension, in which salient properties of the vehicle are transferred to the topic. Instead, four-year-olds seem to be calling to mind salient properties for *either* term (rather than for the vehicle) and then applying these to the other term to determine if there is a match.

Unfortunately, this study did not include adults as subjects. Thus, we do not know whether sensitivity to asymmetry leads to greater difficulty with ground identification in the case of metaphors in reverse order, in which the ground is more salient to the topic than the vehicle. It is possible that adults would perform equally well on both orders. This need not mean that they are insensitive to the asymmetry of metaphor. Rather, given a metaphor in the "wrong" order, they may reverse the order mentally before identifying the ground.

Even if both orders are equally comprehensible, however,

subjects may take longer to understand the reversed order; or they may prefer the "correct" order, finding it more sensible. A better test would use metaphors whose reversal either alters the ground (as in "Surgeons are butchers") or those whose reversal renders the metaphor nonsensical ("Your face is an open book"). Moreover, subjects should be asked not only to give interpretations of the metaphors but also to indicate their preferences.

Had Piaget conducted his study of proverb comprehension using nonmetalinguistic response measures and a rich context, he would most likely have found that children have the competence to understand proverbs by the preschool years. Indeed, a study by Honeck and associates (1980) demonstrated just that. Nonetheless, the point remains that when children do err in understanding metaphors, they typically err at step 3. They know not to take the utterance as is and manage to infer an unstated meaning using the principle of similarity. Where they stumble is in discovering the appropriate match to what is said given the context.

The fact that children infer the wrong meaning given a relational, nonsensory metaphor raises the question of the source of this error. There are at least two possibilities. On the one hand, children may be incapable of perceiving the kinds of similarities on which nonsensory metaphors are based. On the other hand, failure may be due simply to insufficient knowledge of the vehicle and/or topic domain, thus limiting the kinds of connections between topic and vehicle that children can perceive.

Support for the first hypothesis would lead to the conclusion that metaphoric ability is not fully developed until the middle childhood years. Without the capacity to perceive nonsensory similarities, children could grasp metaphors based on sensory similarities, but would be inherently incapable of grasping those based on nonsensory links.

Support for the second hypothesis would suggest that what develops and enables metaphor comprehension is not anything inherent to metaphoric ability but rather something extrinsic to it. Metaphoric ability may be present at the onset of language acquisition and may reveal itself whenever the child has enough knowledge of the elements being linked, even if the ground is nonsensory. If knowledge is at the root of difficulty with non-sensory metaphors, we would still expect children to grasp sensory metaphors earlier, since children know more about physical than relational attributes of things. Knowledge of relational aspects of objects can only be acquired through experience; physical aspects are known directly through the senses.

Since both hypotheses are consistent with the finding of greater relative difficulty with nonsensory (than sensory) metaphors, we must look elsewhere for evidence to discriminate between these hypotheses. One method is to examine non-metaphoric tasks for evidence about the kinds of similarities that children can (or cannot) perceive. A second is to investigate the effect of knowledge about the topic and vehicle domains on comprehension. These two lines of evidence should reveal whether comprehension failure is due to lack of an ability at the core of metaphor comprehension (similarity perception) or to lack of an ability more extrinsic to metaphor comprehension (domain knowledge).

· Chapter 4 ·

Constraints on
Metaphor Comprehension

A four-year-old child can immediately comprehend a description of clouds as pillows. Children of this age are quite capable of explaining that clouds are not really pillows, and that what the speaker means is that clouds are white and fluffy like pillows. But ask this same child whether a cloud is a sponge, and puzzlement or denial will ensue. The child may express even greater bewilderment if asked whether a sad memory can be like a cloud.

Certain kinds of metaphors seem to prove more difficult than others, even when factors such as context and response mode are controlled. Two rival hypotheses have been proposed to account for these differences. One explanation points to a perceptual or conceptual deficit: children's similarity perception abilities may not be fully developed, and this limits the kinds of grounds they can perceive. The types of similarity that a child cannot yet perceive or understand should then predict the types of metaphor that will be incomprehensible. Note that the cloud-pillow metaphor is based on sensory similarity, whereas the cloud-sponge and cloud-sad metaphors are based on non-sensory similarities. Clouds and sponges do not look alike but both hold water (a relational, or functional, similarity); and clouds and sadness are alike only in that they are both negatively valenced (a psychological-physical similarity). Perhaps children's difficulty with metaphors of the cloud-sponge and cloud-sad variety is due to an inability to recognize nonsensory similarity.

An alternative hypothesis points to an informational rather than a perceptual-conceptual deficit and suggests that children's *domain knowledge,* rather than their similarity perception abilities, is underdeveloped. *Domain* is the term used to refer to categories (in part culturally determined) by which we organize our world—categories such as furniture, vehicles, personality traits, and so on. By *domain knowledge* I mean knowledge about the internal structure of a domain, how it functions, and the boundaries that delimit it. To understand a metaphor one must know something about the domains involved. Although very young children have the competence to perceive all of the kinds of similarities that adults perceive, they may lack articulated knowledge of the domains from which either the topic or vehicle is drawn, and thus fail to see the similarity between the topic and vehicle. One cannot know which aspects of the vehicle domain to map onto the topic domain if little is known about one or both domains. Hence, the bewilderment that may occur when a child hears a metaphor. On this account, the confusion has nothing to do with an inability to recognize the similarity underlying the metaphor.

Underdeveloped domain knowledge may also lead to false interpretation. If children have not yet formed a distinction between two domains (those of animate and inanimate objects, for example), then metaphors linking such domains are taken literally. The child then shows that "illusion of understanding" described by Piaget (1974) in his study of proverbs.

In this chapter I consider both hypotheses in turn, first investigating similarity perception skills, to determine whether there might be certain classes of similarity that are inaccessible in early childhood; and then addressing whether misunderstanding metaphor could be due to a deficit in knowledge about the domain of the topic or vehicle. If children fail to understand metaphors because they lack the ability to grasp certain classes of nonliteral similarity, we must conclude that it is metaphoric ability per se that is underdeveloped. But if children only fail because they lack knowledge of the world, we can then conclude that metaphoric ability is present at least as early as we can test for it.

Kinds of Similarity

There is no limit to the kinds of similarities, or grounds, on which a metaphor can be based. Although any attempt to classify kinds of similarity may be philosophically suspect (Goodman, 1976), such an attempt is necessary if we are to investigate the kinds of metaphoric similarities perceivable by the young child.

• *Sensory Similarity*

There are at least five different classes of sensory similarity (see Bornstein, 1984).

(1) The similarity between different views of the same object.

(2) The similarity between one object and its two-dimensional representation.

(3) The similarity between information about an object conveyed in one sensory modality and information about the same object conveyed in another sensory modality. For example, if we see something without touching it, and later touch it without seeing it, we can recognize it as the same (or a similar) object.

(4) The similarity between two stimuli perceived within the same sensory modality, such as two objects that are both round or blue (static similarity) or that both roll or wiggle (dynamic similarity).

(5) The similarity between certain stimuli perceived through two different sensory modalities. A bright orange neon light is perceived as more similar to a loud scream than to a whisper; a pale gray light is more like a whisper than a scream; the sound of a sneeze is perceived as brighter than the sound of a cough (Marks, 1982a). The ability to perceive cross-sensory similarity is commonly referred to as *synesthesia*. The weak form of synesthesia, possessed universally, enables us to make judgments

about how two sensory domains are aligned. In contrast, for those rare individuals who possess the strong form of synesthesia, the two sensory domains are fused rather than aligned, and hence sneeze sounds actually *look* brighter than cough sounds. This fifth type of similarity is perhaps the most "abstract" form of sensory similarity since there is no measurable physical similarity between the elements linked. Nonetheless, it is classified here as sensory rather than nonsensory because it is based on perceived similarities between different sensory experiences.

These kinds of sensory similarity can be grouped in two ways: according to whether the similarity exists between two perceptions of the same object (as in the first three), or between two different objects (as in the fourth and fifth); and according to whether the similarity is perceived within modalities (as in the first, second, and fourth), or across modalities (as in the third and fifth). Sensory metaphors are based on the fourth and fifth types of similarity. In what follows, I call such metaphors *within-modality* and *cross-modality* metaphors, respectively.

Within-modality metaphors link objects perceived within the same sensory modality, as in "Clouds are pillows" (sight); "The wind is a lion" (sound); "The leaves are dancers" (movement, sight); "His beard was sandpaper" (touch). Whenever a metaphor links two elements on the basis of similarity in shape, sound, color, motion, texture, smell, or some combination of these, it can be considered to be a within-modality metaphor. These metaphors are very common and are used in the service of physical description. The following poem (found in an anthology of poems for children) is filled with such sensory metaphors:

> This wind brings all dead things to life,
> *Branches that lash the air like whips*
> And dead leaves rolling in a hurry
> Or peering in a rabbit's bury
> Or trying to push down a tree;
> Gates that fly open to the wind
> And close again behind,

And fields that are a flowing sea
And make the cattle look like ships;
Straws glistening and stiff
Lying on air as on a shelf
And pond that leaps to leave itself;
And feathers too that rise and float,
Each feather changed into a bird.

(Andrew Young, "A Windy Day"; italics mine)

By contrast, *cross-modality metaphors* link stimuli perceived across different sensory modalities. They are based on the links connecting bright colors and loud sounds, high pitches and small sizes, muted colors and quiet sounds, and so on. The following fragment from a poem by Michael Ryan provides a nice example:

. . . the brawny, red-haired Orthodox priest,
whose *shaggy orange beard* over his black-smocked chest
was like an *explosion* from a dark doorway
of a *wild, high-pitched laugh.*   ("Tourists on Paros"; italics mine)

In this case the metaphoric connection is between a flame-colored, unkempt beard and an explosion of a wild, high-pitched laugh. Marks (1982b) provides many more examples from poetry: brightness and loudness are linked in "the dawn came up like thunder" (Rudyard Kipling) and "sunlight above roars like a vast sea" (Conrad Aiken); muted colors and quiet are linked in "The murmur of the gray twilight" (Edgar Allan Poe); and sharpness and high pitch are linked in "the silver needle-note of a fife" (J. Auslander).

Apparently many of the cross-modality metaphors found in poetry (at least French and English poetry) are based on only a few synesthetic resemblances (Marks, 1975, 1978). But one need not go to poetry to find examples of cross-modality metaphors, for they permeate our language: we speak of garish colors as "loud" and "sharp," muted colors as "quiet" and "soft," low tones as "dark" and "heavy," high-pitched tones as "thin" and "tiny," and so on. These cross-modal resemblances are universally perceived (Marks, 1978), despite the fact that the links are between stimuli in two different sensory channels.

• *Nonsensory Similarity*

Resemblances may also be based on information that is entirely nonsensory, and it is impossible to come up with an exhaustive taxonomy of all of the varieties of nonsensory similarities. Such similarities are, perhaps, best defined by what they are not—all those similarities that are not apprehended by our senses. As Rosch (1973) has suggested, it is nonsensory similarity that links members within a *superordinate* category (such as various kinds of animals) since members of categories at this level often do not resemble one another at all (in contrast to members of a *basic object level* category such as collies, retrievers, and German shepherds, all of which belong to the basic object level category "dog").

The similarity between elements normally classified in separate superordinate categories, such as a fox (animal) and a thief (human), often forms the ground of a nonsensory metaphor. The most common kinds of nonsensory metaphors are called here *relational* and *psychological-physical* metaphors. To call a cloud a sponge is to make a relational metaphor (see Carbonell, 1982; Gentner, 1983); to call a memory a cloud is to make a psychological-physical metaphor. As will become apparent, the boundary between these two types of nonsensory metaphor is fuzzy at best.

Relational metaphors are based on similarities between objects, situations, or events that are physically dissimilar, but, owing to parallel internal structures, function in a similar way: clouds and sponges, for example, which function to hold and then release water. Thus when we speak of the mind as a computer, we mean that the mind operates on information in the same way as a computer does. And when we speak of family roots, we are thinking of the similarity between the roots of a tree, which anchor it to the ground and provide it with sustenance, and family origins, which link a person to his past and provide him with a sense of identity. Both of these are relational metaphors. (With regard to the argument against the simple substitution view of metaphor, note how difficult it is to paraphrase adequately a simple, succinct metaphor such as "family roots.") When we liken someone's face to an open book, we mean not that the face is physically similar to a book, but rather that they both function in the same way, revealing their secrets for all to see. There is no physical similarity involved here, only a highly abstract kind of resemblance between two kinds of objects. When T. S. Eliot writes, in "The Love Song of J. Alfred Prufrock," "When the evening is spread out against the sky / Like a patient etherised upon a table," he offers us another example: darkness lies still covering the sky the way a flattened patient lies still covering the operating table.

Psychological-physical metaphors are based on a resemblance between sensory attributes of a physical object (perceived through any sensory modality) and psychological, non-sensory attributes of a person. Perhaps the most common instances of psychological-physical metaphors are those used to describe personality traits. (These were the kinds studied by Asch and Nerlove, 1960, and by Winner and colleagues, 1976.) We speak, for example, of stubborn people as "hard," cheerful people as "sunny," cranky people as "sour," and dishonest people as "slippery" or "crooked." We also describe moods as "warm," "heated," "icy," and so on.

It is often difficult to articulate the grounds of psychological-physical metaphors. But the fact that such metaphoric descriptions of personality traits exist in similar form in historically unrelated languages (Asch, 1955) is evidence that these metaphors are not based on arbitrary mappings determined by the culture. Most people intuitively feel that there is a similarity between the structure of certain physical domains and the structure of certain personality traits and affective states, even though they may not be able to explain just what this similarity is.

In poetry, psychological-physical metaphors may take a somewhat more complex form than the simple application of an adjective to a person or to a human behavior. Consider another line from Michael Ryan's "Tourists on Paros": "But if you also suddenly feel the loss snap open beneath like a well covered with grass . . ." Here, the sudden intrusion of a memory of an emotional loss is aligned with the sensation of unexpected loss of physical support. Shakespeare's implicit comparison between psychological turmoil and knitting that has come unravelled ("Sleep that knits up the raveled sleave of care") is yet another example of this form.

The distinction between relational and psychological-physical metaphors is often vague. For instance, is the link between computer (physical object) and mind (psychological "object") relational or psychological-physical? I have classified it here as relational, choosing to limit psychological-physical metaphors to descriptions of personality traits and mood states. This distinction will prove useful in investigating children's understanding of metaphor, but I do not wish to claim that the distinction is either clear or necessary.

Children's Perception of Similarity

Evidence for the kinds of similarity children can perceive has come from three areas of research: infant perception, lexical acquisition, and classification skills.

• Infant Perception

Infants have been shown to perceive all five kinds of sensory similarity discussed above (Bornstein, 1984). Inborn object constancy allows infants to recognize a bottle seen from one angle as the same bottle seen from another angle (Bower, 1974); they can perceive pictures as representations of objects (Deloache, Strauss, and Maynard, 1979; Hochberg and Brooks, 1962); they are capable of mapping tactile information about an object onto visual information about the same object (Gottfried, Rose, and Bridger, 1977); they can readily grasp within-modality similarities, such as color and shape (see, for example, Bornstein, Kessen, and Weiskopf, 1976; Riccutti, 1965); and they can even perceive cross-modality similarities.

Let us consider the evidence for cross-modality perception in infancy, since cross-modality similarity is the most abstract kind of sensory similarity and one of the two kinds of sensory similarity that underlie metaphor. Infants can match a film of a ball bouncing with the sound of hands clapping in the same rhythm (Spelke, 1976); neonates perceive loud sounds and bright lights as similar (Lewkowicz and Turkewitz, 1980); and nine- to twelve-month-olds perceive visual patterns, such as a dotted line, as more similar to a discontinuous than a continuous sound (Wagner et al., 1981).

The ability of infants to match visual and auditory events appears to be metaphoric. Infants seem to be overriding the boundary between visual and auditory experiences when they match a dotted line to a discontinuous sound. But are they in fact overriding a boundary between modalities, or are their primary categories amodal to begin with? This question was investigated by Wagner and associates (1982) using a dishabituation paradigm. Infants were presented with a discontinuous sound until they became bored with this stimulus (as measured by decrease in heart rate). They were then presented with either a discontinuous line or a continuous sound, and their heart rate was measured. An increase in heart rate indicated that the infant was renewing interest, and a renewal of interest was seen to show that the infant perceived the second stimulus as different from the initial (now boring) stimulus. Surprisingly, infants who had become habituated to the *discontinuous sound* renewed their interest more often in response to the continuous *sound* than in response to the *discontinuous* line. This indicates that they perceived more similarity between the discontinuous sound and line (a cross-modality connection) than between two kinds of sound (a within-modality connection). The finding suggests that some amodal synesthetic categories may be primary for infants. If so, recognizing a similarity between discontinuous auditory and visual events is not an act of metaphoric perception because it involves no overriding of a primary category boundary. The infant is not grouping two elements that he normally perceives as dissimilar, but is simply revealing his primary, amodal classification system. These early amodal categories, however, provide the raw material for metaphor comprehension later on.

• *Lexical Acquisition*

Studies of lexical acquisition have demonstrated that children overextend words primarily on the basis of sensory (especially static visual) attributes of objects (Anglin, 1977; Barrett, 1978; Bowerman, 1976; Clark, 1973; Thomson and Chapman, 1976). The dimension of shape seems to be a particularly potent perceptual attribute: thus, round shapes are called "balls," four-legged creatures with tails are called "dogs," and squiggles are called "snakes." Children are more likely to use static perceptual features (such as shape) than dynamic perceptual features (such as movement) as the bases for their overextensions.

Although static perceptual similarities underlie most early lexical categories (Clark, 1983), there is some evidence for overextensions on the basis of nonsensory similarities. Some overextensions are based on function—what one can do with an object (Nelson, 1974). Anything that can be thrown, whether or not it is round, may be called "ball." Others are based on the feelings that the referents elicit in the child (Bowerman, 1976, 1977; Nelson et al., 1978; Rescorla, 1980). Bowerman (1977) reported that her daughter used the term "too tight" to refer to any situation in which she felt physically constrained, including having to submit to having her ears washed or having her chin held when she was given medicine. Words may also be extended on the basis of the child's spatial relationship to the referents, rather than on the basis of any inherent physical features of the referent. Thus, Piaget (1962) noted that his fourteen-month-old daughter called all things seen from her balcony "bow wow," presumably because she had first learned the word when looking at a dog from her balcony. And I observed my one-year-old son apply the term "uh-oh" to anything that needed to be fixed or required adult intervention—a hangnail, a dirty diaper, a toy dropped out of reach, a broken cookie, and so on. Evidence from various lexical acquisition studies shows that while children tend to use static perceptual features as the bases of their lexical extensions (Anglin, 1977; Barrett, 1978; Clark, 1973, 1983), they are capable of using nonsensory, functional features as well.

• *Classification Skills*

According to traditional research on classification (Inhelder and Piaget, 1964; Vygotsky, 1962), preschoolers are unable to use a consistent criterion in sorting objects that vary along several physical dimensions (such as size, color, and shape). Instead of sorting the objects by shape, for instance, the child might place a square and a triangle together because they make a configuration like a house and roof—a classification Inhelder and Piaget (1964) called a "graphic collection."

Other researchers as well have found support for the claim that preschoolers use classification principles different from those used by adults. Whereas adults classify taxonomically (by conventional category), preschoolers have been shown to classify on the basis of spatial relations between objects and also on the basis of associations, chain complexes, or stories that seem to link the various objects grouped together (Annett, 1959; Bruner, Olver, and Greenfield, 1966). When preschoolers do classify by similarity, often the grouping is only partially made on this basis.

But are children of this age unable or simply disinclined to use a consistent principle of similarity in object sorting tasks? More recent research clearly shows that preschoolers have the ability to classify consistently on the basis of similarity. Asked to sort objects into superordinate categories (for example, chairs, tables, and couches into the category "furniture"), three-year-olds fail and four-year-olds succeed (Rosch et al., 1976). But asked to sort objects at the basic object level (kitchen chairs, living room chairs, and rocking chairs into the category "chairs"), even three-year-olds demonstrate the ability to sort taxonomically, putting the chairs together and separating them from the tables.

What is special about categories at the basic object level is that category members share clusters of attributes and parts and elicit similar motor movements, whereas at the superordinate level members share fewer attributes (Rosch et al., 1976). (For example, chairs have seats, legs, and backs, and are for sitting on; chairs and tables are both furniture but do not both have seats, backs, or a common function.) Members of a basic object level category are therefore similar in shape (a sensory similarity) and in function (a nonsensory similarity).

Because of the perceptual and functional commonalities among members of basic level categories, children can learn to form such categories through perception (noticing similarities in shape) and through action (interacting with members in the same way). Thus, it is not surprising that the boundaries separating basic level categories should be among the first distinctions children make in the world of objects. When a dishabituation paradigm is used—which is more sensitive than a sorting task—children as young as one to two years show sensitivity to superordinate categories such as furniture, food, and animals (Ross, 1980). Further evidence for the ability of children to classify by similarity comes from Markman and Hutchinson (1984), who found that two-year-olds extend newly learned nouns to objects related categorically rather than taxonomically.

The findings in the three areas discussed above demonstrate that children are capable of perceiving both sensory and nonsensory similarities, at least by the time they begin to acquire language. There is thus reason to expect that even preschool children ought to understand both sensory and nonsensory metaphors—that is, if all that is required is the ability to perceive the kind of similarity underlying the metaphor.

Children's Perception of Metaphors

• *Within-Modality Metaphors*

Metaphors grounded in one sensory modality are well within the grasp of preschool children. This has been demonstrated in a number of studies. For example, Winner, McCarthy, and

Gardner (1980) tested children aged three, four, and five (as well as eight and ten, and adults) on their abilities to apply physically based metaphoric names to presented objects. For a judgment task, children were shown objects such as blocks of various shapes, odd kitchen gadgets, a clothespin, crayons, and so on, and were offered three possible "pretend" names for each object: the object's literal name, an anomalous name (calling a mop held upside down a "toaster"), and a metaphoric name based on sensory similarity (calling the upside down mop a "flower"—the similarity being shape or configuration). Children were then asked to select the best pretend name. In a correction task children were to listen to a puppet offering either metaphoric or anomalous pretend names for the objects, decide in each case whether the names were "good" or "silly," and, if silly, offer a better one. The metaphoric names used in both conditions were based on resemblances of shape, color, texture, movement, and sound.

Even the three-year-olds were able to select the metaphoric name and to judge the metaphoric names superior to the anomalous ones. The scores, once chance level performance had been accounted for, showed that 15% of three-year-olds' responses chose the metaphoric name, and that 24% of their responses to the correction task were correct. The respective figures for four-year-olds were 61% and 40%; for five-year-olds, 81% and 56%; and for eight- and ten-year-olds, higher yet. Although three-year-olds did demonstrate some sensitivity to sensory metaphors, they also revealed that they did not understand such metaphors nearly as readily as children even one year older. Moreover, in the correction task three- and four-year-olds were more likely to accept a metaphoric name ("rocketship" for cone-shaped block) than to reject an anomalous one ("fire engine" for cone-shaped block). Thus they proved less sensitive to anomaly than did older subjects. Nonetheless, three-year-olds showed that they have the capacity to comprehend within-modality sensory metaphors.

All we can conclude from this study, in which children were given the objects and were asked to match them to a metaphoric name, is that children can understand a sensory metaphoric name for an object when that object is physically present. But what about a situation, perhaps more true to life, in which a metaphor is used to refer to an *absent* object? Can children work out the relevant similarity between two objects when one of these must be recalled from memory? Other studies have shown that preschoolers are capable of understanding within-modality metaphors even in the absence of the objects described. For instance, Shantiris (1983) found that kindergartners can distinguish anomalous sentences from metaphors such as "Eyes are marbles." In this study children were asked not to explain the metaphors, but simply to decide in each case whether the sentence made sense. Children were significantly more likely to accept the metaphors than the anomalies. This finding can only be explained by children's recognition of the similarity underlying the metaphors.

In another study (which unfortunately did not include children younger than age six), children were asked to finish incomplete similes such as "Tangled hair is like . . ." (Mendelsohn, Gardner, and Winner, 1981). Children were given three choices: a within-modality metaphoric choice ("boiled spaghetti heaped in a bowl"), an associative choice ("a plastic comb"), and an anomalous choice ("a teddy bear on a shelf"). Children as young as age six had no trouble selecting the metaphoric names based on visual similarity, averaging 3.7 correct responses out of a possible 5.

The literature on early lexical development reveals a predominance of overextensions based on static sensory features of objects rather than on either dynamic sensory features (such as how an object moves) or on functional features (Clark, 1983). If this indicates that children most readily recognize static sensory similarities, then we might predict that static sensory metaphors should be more readily understood than those based on dynamic sensory features. Surprisingly, however, just the opposite is true. The relative ease of perceiving a nonverbal metaphoric similarity based on static as opposed to dynamic sensory features of objects was investigated by Dent (1984). In this study children aged five, seven, and ten saw triads of brief color films

of familiar objects or activities. One triad, for instance, con-
sisted of a ballerina spinning, a top spinning, and a ballerina
leaping. Two members of each triad were metaphorically related (ballerina and top); two showed objects that belonged to
the same conventional category (ballerina spinning and ballerina leaping), and two had no clear relationship (ballerina
leaping and top spinning).

Half of the metaphoric matches were based on similarities
between moving objects (as in the triad above), and half were
based on similarities between stationary objects (a wrinkled
face and a wrinkled apple). The movements used in the metaphoric pairings were spinning (ballerina and top), leaping (deer
and dancer), bucking (car and horse), and waving (hands and
wheat). The static properties used in the metaphoric pairings
were height (tall building and giraffe), texture (wrinkled face
and wrinkled apple, posture (proud lion and proud king), and
color and position (white moon and white kite). Each triad of
films was presented simultaneously on a screen, in a triangular
formation, and children were asked to "pick two that go together." Although literal pairings were more frequent than
metaphoric pairings in responses from five- and seven-year-olds
(which is not surprising, given the instructions), children of all
ages were more likely to make metaphoric pairings linking moving than stationary objects.

Hence, it appears that visually apprehended commonalities in
movement create more accessible kinds of within-modality sensory grounds than do visually perceived commonalities in static
physical properties. But one must be cautious in drawing such a
conclusion on the basis of the few items used here. There were
no metaphoric pairings based on the stationary property of
shape (except for a practice item), for instance; and given the
predominance of early lexical overextensions and spontaneous
metaphors based on shape (Clark, 1973; Winner, 1979), triads
with shape similarities built in might have yielded the highest
performances of all.

Further support for Dent's conclusion that dynamic sensory
grounds are more accessible than static ones comes from a study

by Calhoun (1984), in which four- and five-year-olds were asked to discriminate between metaphoric and anomalous sentences. The metaphoric sentences were grounded either in static sensory features ("Clouds are like flying ice cream"), dynamic sensory features ("A snowflake is like a ballerina"), or non-sensory similarities ("Old school teachers are like encyclopedias"). Children heard each metaphor along with a corresponding anomaly ("Clouds are like flying boxes"; "A snowflake is like a school"; "Old school teachers are like stoves") and were asked to pick the one most "true" or "real." They were also asked to explain the metaphors.

On the task involving discrimination between anomaly and metaphor, children performed better with metaphors based on movement than with those based on static sensory features. Surprisingly, children performed at chance level on the static sensory items, and hence performed better on the nonsensory than the static sensory items. This finding conflicts with many studies showing that young children can perceive metaphors grounded in static sensory features (Shantiris, 1983; Winner, McCarthy, and Gardner, 1980) and thus suggests that the sensory metaphors used were too difficult. Indeed, some of the sensory metaphors used, such as "A dream is like a movie," and "A butterfly is a winged rainbow," do appear to be difficult.

When subjects were asked to explain the metaphors, a different order of difficulty was revealed: movement metaphors were explained correctly more often than static ones (mirroring the discrimination results); but in contrast to the results of the discrimination task, those based on nonsensory similarity proved most difficult of all to explain. This finding indicates once again that an explanation task may underestimate the child's level of comprehension.

The evidence points to the conclusion that young children are capable of understanding within-modality metaphors, and that they understand metaphors based on dynamic features more readily than those based on static sensory features. Perhaps children perceive a similarity in static sensory features as a case of literal similarity, and a similarity in movement as a case of nonliteral similarity. This is an issue open to investigation: discrepancies between the findings from studies of lexical overextensions and of metaphor comprehension need to be accounted for.

• *Cross-Modality Metaphors*

Metaphors grounded in certain types of cross-modality similarity prove no more difficult for children to understand than those grounded in within-modality similarity. This is not surprising, given that even infants have been shown capable of perceiving links between brightness and loudness (Lewkowicz and Turkewitz, 1980), and between discontinuous lines and sounds (Wagner et al., 1981).

Marks, Hammeal, and Bornstein (in press) explored children's ability to make nonverbal cross-modal matches and to understand verbal metaphors based on such grounds. The children tested were between four and thirteen years of age. The nonverbal task required them to align pitches of varying degrees of loudness with lights of varying brightness levels. The verbal task required children to listen to metaphors such as "sunlight whispers," "sunlight roars," "moonlight whispers," and "moonlight roars," and to rate the nouns for brightness and loudness. (Roaring light ought to be rated as brighter than whispering light; and any kind of sunlight should be louder than moonlight.)

Children as young as four years of age succeeded on these tasks, although the distinctions they made were not as fine as those noted by adults. Nonetheless, the important finding is that at least by age four, children know that loud and high pitches are brighter than quiet and low pitches, and that bright objects are loud and high in pitch, whereas dimly colored objects are quiet and low in pitch. Moreover, children are not only able to perceive the similarity between two perceptually given stimuli, as demonstrated by their performance on the nonverbal task.

They are also able to perceive such cross-modal similarities when they are coded linguistically, as demonstrated by their performance on the verbal task.

Not all of the cross-modal connections proved equally accessible to young children. When the connection to be made was between pitch and brightness, children had no difficulty at all, although they performed slightly better on the perceptual than the verbal task. On the perceptual matching task, 94% of the responses from four- and five-year-olds were correct, a figure no different from that for adults. On the verbal task, 74% of their responses were correct.

Next in ease of understanding were connections between loudness and brightness. On the perceptual task, 74% of the responses from four- and five-year-olds were correct, but on the verbal task, children that age performed at chance level. (The ability to perceive the connection between loudness and brightness was also demonstrated by Gardner, 1974, who asked three- and four-year-olds to project the terms "loud" and "quiet" onto color swatches, and by Lewkowicz and Turkewitz, 1980, with neonates.)

Latest to emerge was the ability to make alignments between pitch and size. This ability did not manifest itself until eleven years of age, suggesting that the connection between high pitch and small size, and between low pitch and large size, may have to be learned (perhaps by noting associations of size and resonance). Hence, certain cross-modal similarities may be detectable at birth and based on neurological substrates; others, whether arbitrary or based on some physical principles, may be available only through learning.

• *Nonsensory Metaphors*

Some studies have suggested that young children find sensory metaphors more accessible than metaphors based on nonsensory similarities. In one such study Gentner and Stuart (1983) presented children aged five and six (as well as older children aged nine to ten, and adults) with three kinds of metaphors:

within-modality (called "attribute" metaphors by Gentner and Stuart), relational, and based on both kinds of similarity. The within-modality metaphors included "A cloud is like a marsh-mallow" (color, shape, softness), "A snake is like a hose" (shape), and "The sun is like an orange" (color and shape). The relational metaphors included "A camera is like a tape re-corder" (both record events to reexperience later), and "Tree bark is like skin" (both are thin layers covering a surface). An example of the dual-grounded metaphors used is "Plant stems are like drinking straws" (both suck up water, and both are long and cylindrical in shape). The task was to provide a verbal interpretation of these sentences.

Despite the fact that the task of paraphrasing is a metalin-guistic one, five-year-olds had no difficulty explaining the simi-larity underlying the sensory metaphors. In fact, they performed as well as adults. The only developmental difference found was that these children offered fewer relational interpretations for both the relational and the dual-grounded metaphors than did older children. This suggests that children had more difficulty perceiving (or at least explaining) relational than sensory simi-larities.

Other studies have also reported greater difficulty with non-sensory than sensory metaphors. For instance, in the 1981 study by Mendelsohn and colleagues discussed earlier, children had to complete (given multiple choices) different kinds of similes (be-sides single modality sensory ones), including those based on relational and psychological-physical grounds; in other words, including those of the form "Tangled hair is like words with letters all mixed up," and "Tangled hair is like a confused idea." Children of all ages selected more appropriate comple-tions when the ground was sensory than when it was nonsen-sory.

Shantiris's (1983) study, also described above, provides us with further evidence for the possibly greater difficulty of psy-chological-physical (but not relational) nonsensory grounds. In her study children not only had to distinguish sensory meta-phors from anomalies, they also had to distinguish relational and psychological-physical metaphors from anomalies. At all ages, children accepted considerably fewer psychological-physical metaphors as comprehensible than they did sensory metaphors. Relational metaphors, however, seemed to pose no more difficulty than did sensory metaphors, for any age group.

In contrast, several studies have found no advantage for sensory over nonsensory metaphors. For example, Kogan and associates (1980) found that children were able to pair metaphorically related pictures that were linked by nonsensory similarity (an aging man and a melted down candle) as easily as pictures linked by single modality sensory similarity (a coiled snake and a winding river). In another study, taking care to control for knowledge of the objects referred to in the metaphors, Nippold, Leonard, and Kail (1984) examined seven-year-olds' ability to understand sensory and psychological-physical metaphors. In their most conservative analyses, no difference was found between the two types of metaphor. (Unfortunately for our purposes, they did not test children aged six and younger.)

Further evidence for the ability of very young children to understand nonsensory metaphoric grounds comes from the metaphors produced in spontaneous speech (discussed in Chapter 5). Although early metaphors tend to be based on sensory grounds, nonsensory grounds have also been noted. Gentner and Stuart (1983) report that a three-year-old child described a new blanket as "full of gas" and an old worn-out blanket as "out of gas." The four-year-old daughter of a friend of mine remarked on the similarity between a sympathetic physical pain (her mother said her arm hurt when she watched her daughter get a shot) and a sympathetic psychological pain (the child had felt sad for her grandmother when the grandmother was sad). And another four-year-old, whose father had just died, seemed to gain insight into the irreversibility of death when a balloon she was holding soared forever out of reach, prompting her to sob for her father (Moore, 1986). (See also Crisafi and Brown, 1983; Gentner, 1977; Holyoak, Junn, and Billman, 1984).

If preschoolers have the ability to perceive nonsensory similarity, how can we explain the results reported by Gentner and

Stuart (1983) and Mendelsohn and colleagues (1981), who found that sensory metaphors were easier to comprehend than at least some kinds of nonsensory metaphors? The most reasonable explanation is that difficulty in understanding nonsensory metaphors has to do with lack of knowledge of the functions of things in the world and not with any deficit in similarity perception. One does not need knowledge of the world to understand sensory metaphors because these are based on similarities apprehendable by perception alone. But to understand nonsensory metaphors, one needs knowledge of the domains in question. For instance, in Gentner and Stuart's study children might not have known about the function of plant stems. Not knowing that stems draw water up from the ground, they cannot be expected to understand a metaphor based on this function. Gentner and Stuart present one piece of evidence in favor of this "domain knowledge" explanation. Before being asked to interpret the similes, children in their study were asked simply to describe each of the objects involved (plant stem, tree bark, skin, and so on). With age, there was a strong increase in the sheer number of properties listed for each object, suggesting that older children bring more world knowledge to bear on their interpretations of metaphors. Greater knowledge of the domains involved makes it more likely that a nonsensory mapping will be understood. Thus, comprehension of nonsensory grounds is more difficult to demonstrate than comprehension of sensory mappings only because the former often requires more knowledge.

Domain Knowledge

To test the hypothesis that problems in metaphor comprehension are the result of limited domain knowledge, one would need to use nonsensory metaphors based on domains highly familiar to children (such as "Friends are like magnets"). This is precisely what was done by Keil (1985), who showed that when knowledge deficits do not intrude, children demonstrate no difficulty in understanding nonsensory metaphors.

Keil (1979, 1985) has argued that comprehension of metaphor depends not only on a familiarity with the referents of the topic and vehicle, but also on an awareness of each of the larger domains to which the topic and vehicle belong. By virtue of juxtaposing terms from two different domains, a metaphor also brings into juxtaposition the two domains themselves. Hence, to understand how the two terms of the metaphor are aligned, one must have some understanding of how the two domains are aligned (see also Kittay and Lehrer, 1981; Tourangeau and Sternberg, 1981).

To illustrate the importance of domain knowledge in metaphor comprehension, let us consider the problem of understanding what it means to call someone "smooth." In order to understand this psychological-physical metaphor, one needs to know something about the domain of textures—that surfaces can be rough, slippery, soft, and hard, as well as smooth. One also needs to know something about the domain of personality types that may correspond to kinds of textures—relaxed, tense, rude, polite, kind, mean, dishonest, poised, awkward, and so on. In other words, one must know what kinds of textures contrast with "smooth," and one must possess fine enough differentiations in the psychological domain to be able to map various textures each onto a different personality type. It follows that once one understands the structures of two given domains, one ought to have the capacity to understand appropriate metaphors based on links between many members of the two domains. That is, once one understands what it means to call a person "smooth," one ought also to understand what it means to call a person "rough," "slippery," "soft," and "hard."

Keil (1985) tested the hypothesis that metaphor understanding emerges on a domain-by-domain basis. This hypothesis is contrasted to the traditional assumption (made, for example, by Asch and Nerlove, 1960; Johnson, 1982; Winner, Rosenstiel, and Gardner, 1976) that metaphor comprehension is a general ability, possessed to greater or lesser extents, which cuts across domains. Keil hypothesized that once it can be established that children understand the structure of two domains, any metaphor bridging these two domains ought to be understandable (provided, that is, that the metaphor to be understood involves a relatively straightforward match along one or two dimensions, and that the terms used are familiar). But understanding of metaphors linking certain domains should not predict understanding of those linking other domains. Keil asked children aged five, eight, and nine to explain metaphors involving eight kinds of domain juxtapositions: (1) animate properties applied to cars ("The car is thirsty/dead/sick"); (2) properties of human vocalizations applied to wind ("The wind whispered/screamed/moaned"); (3) human occupations applied to animals ("The deer is the athlete of the woods"; "The spider is the artist of the woods"; "The beaver is the carpenter of the woods"); (4) properties of plants applied to ideas ("The idea bloomed/wilted/was planted"); (5) eating terms applied to the activity of reading ("The boy tasted/bit into/gobbled up the book"); (6–8) weather, texture, and taste terms applied to personality types ("She was a sunny/stormy/frosty person"; "He was a smooth/scratchy/slippery person"; "She was a sour/bitter/sugary person").

As hypothesized, metaphoric comprehension emerged on a domain-by-domain basis. Once children showed understanding of one metaphor juxtaposing two domains, they understood most metaphors involving the same domains. This was demonstrated by a bimodal distribution of understanding for each type of metaphor: either children understood practically none of the metaphors of a particular type, or they understood all (or almost all) of them. Moreover, children frequently understood all of the metaphors of one type and none of those of another type.

The order in which children differentiate domains was also explored by Keil (1979), and the relative difficulty of the metaphors used in Keil's study was predicted by the order in which children were shown to acquire knowledge of different domains. Children aged five, seven, nine, and eleven were presented with sentences that either made sense ("The rock is heavy") or were anomalous ("The recess is heavy") and were asked to judge the sentences' appropriateness. If a child permitted two terms from different domains to be followed by the same predicates, only one of which was appropriate, Keil concluded that the child had not yet fully differentiated the two domains. For instance, if a child agreed that both a rock and a recess could be heavy, the child revealed that he treated physical objects and events as the same, at least with respect to the attribute "heavy."

Using this procedure, Keil found that preschoolers first distinguish between living things and all other things. In the latter category are events, ideas, and inanimate physical objects, all of which the preschoolers allowed to be heavy and tall (attributes of physical objects only) and an hour long (an attribute of events only). The fact that the primary distinction made by preschoolers was between animate and inanimate objects demonstrates that children of this age do not always think animistically, as Piaget (1929) suggested (see Gelman and Baillargeon, 1983, for further evidence that children are not always animistic).

Older children revealed more differentiated categories. Among seven-year-olds, the categories had doubled to four: animals (which could be "asleep" or "sorry"), plants (which could be "sick" but not "asleep" or "sorry"), inanimate physical objects (which could be "heavy" but not "sick," "asleep," or "sorry"), and nonphysical objects. In the last category were events (such as recess) as well as abstract objects (ideas), both of which could be "an hour long," but not heavy. Further distinctions were shown to be constructed as development proceeds.

These findings have direct applications to metaphor comprehension. Preschool children should be able to understand metaphors which span the first boundary to be differentiated— that between animate and inanimate objects. Metaphors that span boundaries not yet differentiated by the preschooler should be misunderstood as literal statements. That is, children should not get beyond step 1 with these metaphors. Thus, if a four-year-old is told that the car is "dead," he should not take this literally, since such a metaphor violates the boundary between animate and inanimate objects, a boundary that the child respects. But if this same child hears a person described as "smooth," he should take this statement literally since he would not yet have differentiated psychological states and physical objects.

Keil's later (1985) study revealed that the order of acquisition of domain distinctions predicted order of acquisition of metaphor comprehension. Thus, metaphors ascribing animate terms to cars were the earliest to be understood, whereas those ascribing plant terms to ideas, and taste, texture, or weather terms to people were grasped considerably later. The car metaphors span the early acquired distinction between animate and inanimate objects; the plant, taste, texture, and weather metaphors span the late-acquired distinction between psychological and physical domains. An understanding of the distinction between the psychological and physical domains is necessary if one is to avoid literal interpretations of metaphors describing an idea as wilting or a person as smooth. It is not surprising that children have difficulty comprehending these kinds of metaphors and at the same time can understand a metaphor such as "The car is thirsty." In the latter, the distinction bridged is one that the child has already mastered; in the former, the distinction bridged is one not yet mastered.

The fact that extensions of physical terms to people were the hardest to understand suggests that psychological-physical metaphors are the most difficult of all nonsensory metaphors to understand: this may be due either to the lack of a sharp boundary between the physical and psychological domains (as Keil's research suggests) or to incomplete knowledge about psychological traits. Children may fail to understand metaphors of the "smooth person" type because they do not yet make fine enough distinctions among personality traits, or because they do not have a reasonable notion of personality traits at all.

Interestingly, Keil found the same kinds of errors reported by Winner, Rosenstiel, and Gardner (1976) and Johnson (1982). But the kind of error made in response to one type of metaphor did not predict the kind made in response to other types. Within any particular domain Keil found a four-step developmental pattern of comprehension, a pattern that unfolds, he argues, as domain knowledge develops. First, given very limited domain knowledge, metaphors based on these domains were taken literally. A "smooth" person, for instance, was said to be someone who has just shaved; and a "sunny" person was said to be yellow. (This kind of response corresponds to primitive-metaphoric responses in Winner, Rosenstiel, and Gardner, 1976, discussed in the previous chapter.)

Next, children grasped the two different domains involved (psychological and physical), but were unable to align the two domains properly. At this level, a "frosty" person was described as someone who always gives things to the poor; and "idea bloomed" was interpreted to mean that an idea went away and was forgotten. These interpretations show only the most global understanding of which two domains were juxtaposed in the metaphors. (This kind of interpretation corresponds to the inappropriate metaphoric responses in Winner, Rosenstiel, and Gardner, 1976.)

At the third level, the domains were aligned along basic dimensions of potency and evaluation (Osgood, Succi, and Tanenbaum, 1957). A "sour" person was described as not very nice; a "stormy" person as "sad," and a "smooth" person as "nice." (These interpretations also correspond to the inappropriate metaphor responses in Winner, Rosenstiel, and Gardner, 1976.) These examples show that children are sensitive to the positive or negative polarity of the metaphors: sourness and storminess are understood to be negative traits, whereas smoothness is recognized as positive. But because the domains were aligned along only a few global dimensions, children at this level often failed to distinguish among meanings of related metaphors. For instance, "sour," "bitter," and "salty" people were all simply "bad" people.

Finally, at the fourth level, with more differentiated knowledge of the domains in question, children proved able to make precise juxtapositions and hence appropriate interpretations. A "sour" person was seen as someone who does not want to do things; a "smooth" person as someone who takes things without yelling; and an idea "mowed down" as an idea replaced by a better one.

The important point here is that a child might make one type of error for texture-personality metaphors and entirely different errors for animate-car or eating-book metaphors. Thus, any study which claims to show that children of certain ages make certain kinds of errors is probably basing this conclusion on only a limited range of metaphors. There appear to be no general strategies of metaphoric ability that cut across all types of metaphor. Instead, Keil has shown regular strategies of understanding *within* but not across particular kinds of metaphors.

To demonstrate further that misunderstanding of a metaphor is due to inadequate domain knowledge rather than to an inability to align two fully understood domains, Keil asked the children in his study to explain the meanings of the terms used. The definitions given revealed overly simplified meanings. For instance, children defined both "greedy" and "lazy" as "bad." That these simplified definitions were not just due to an inability to articulate word meanings is shown by the fact that the same children had no difficulty defining terms from other, more fully understood domains.

Children's difficulty with understanding nonsensory metaphors is shown by Keil to be a function of lack of sufficient domain knowledge. A study by Cicone, Gardner, and Winner (1981) demonstrated that although some knowledge of the psychological domain is necessary, it is not always sufficient. In this study children were asked to select the most appropriate ending for a story. One story was about a person who always got his own way. In the metaphor task children had to decide whether the story should end with "Billy was a bulldozer" (a psychological-physical metaphor) or with one of two other anomalous endings. In the literal task children had to choose between "Billy was bossy" and two other inappropriate (literal) descriptions. Children proved able to select the appropriate literal descriptions more frequently than the appropriate metaphoric descriptions. This finding shows that even when children grasp the psychological domain (as demonstrated by their selection of the appropriate literal, psychological trait term), they may fail to understand a metaphor linking a psychological trait to a physical object. One possible explanation is that children had insufficient knowledge of the vehicle domain (bulldozers). I think that this is unlikely, however, since the vehicle terms were ones felt to be familiar to young children. It is far more likely that children need a more detailed knowledge of the psychological domain in question than was tested here. To understand what it means to call someone a "bulldozer," children may need to distinguish being bossy from being nasty, angry, conceited, and so on, distinctions that were not included in the multiple choices. If children have only a general idea of what bossy people are like, they will not be able to identify this trait when they hear a person metaphorically described as a bulldozer.

The ability to perceive many of the kinds of similarities that underlie sensory metaphors appears to be inherent in our sensory system, and the ability to perceive nonsensory similarities can be detected as soon as children know enough about the domains being linked. What children lack is not the ability to detect nonsensory similarities, but rather sufficient knowledge of the domains on which nonsensory metaphors are based. Knowledge of the world, though not necessary for recognition of sensory similarities, is a prerequisite for recognition of relational, functional similarities. Thus, verbal metaphors based on innately perceivable sensory similarities are understood at as young an age as can be tested, whereas nonsensory metaphors are only understood if children possess sufficient knowledge of domains in question.

Marks and Bornstein (1985) make the interesting argument that the innate ability to perceive connections between sensory modalities may make possible all later metaphoric ability. The perception of similarity between two different sensory modalities may give the child the idea that two different things can be perceived as similar. By analogy, children may then extend this process to nonsensory domains. But to map nonsensory domains requires articulated knowledge of these categories, which can only be gained through experience with the world.

If children can understand nonsensory metaphors when they have sufficient knowledge of the domains, then they ought to be able to produce nonsensory metaphors given familiarity with the domains. An examination of the types of metaphors that children produce spontaneously should reveal whether comprehension and production develop at the same pace, or whether, as is more often the case in language development, production lags behind comprehension.

Chapter 5

Early Metaphors in Spontaneous Speech

During the preschool years children often use words in unconventional ways, producing phrases and names that they could not have heard from adults (Clark, 1973, 1983). Recall from Piaget (1962) how his daughter, who had initially used the term "bow-wow" to refer to a dog seen from her balcony, then used this term to apply to *all* things seen from her balcony, irrespective of their resemblance to a dog. Guillaume (1927), an early student of child language, provided a similar example when he noted that the label "nénin" was used to refer to many different kinds of round objects: a button, the point of an elbow, an eye, and a face.

Early unconventional names are often quite inventive: "comb" for centipede (Rescorla, 1980); "drooling" for water dripping down from the ceiling; "cornflakes" for freckles; "scar" for a streak of skywriting; "fire engine in my tummy" for stomach ache; "crust" for street curb; "apple" for grape; and "I'm an N" as the child runs up and down the stairs (Winner, unpublished observations).

Children's early literal word usage is related to adult usage in four ways (Clark, 1983). (1) Over half of a child's early words may be overextended, that is, applied too broadly (Rescorla, 1980). An example is the use of "ball" for balls as well as apples, grapes, doorknobs, balloons, and other round objects (Clark, 1973). Overextensions are based on similarity, and hence, like metaphors, offer clues to how children classify the world. When children acquire the correct literal name for an object, its overextended name drops out (Clark, 1983). Thus, once the child acquires the term "apple," she will stop calling it a ball. (2) Some of the child's words are underextended, as when the word "shoes" is used only for the child's sneakers (Anglin, 1977; Reich, 1976). (3) Some early words overlap partially in meaning with adult usage, as in the use of "dog" for big dogs and cows but not small dogs and calves (Clark, 1983). (4) And there is sometimes no connection between a child's word meaning and an adult's meaning, yielding an apparent anomaly. Bowerman (1976) reported one such case, when her daughter used "hi" to refer to anything covering a hand or foot, presumably because her mother had shown her finger puppets and always made the puppets say "hi."

Most relevant for our purposes are overextensions, because these kinds of errors are easily confusable with metaphors. Some researchers have argued that a subset of apparent overextensions may in fact be instances of metaphor (Billow, 1981; Bloom, 1973; Carlson and Anisfeld, 1969; Hudson and Nelson, 1984; Marti, 1979; Nelson et al., 1978; Thomson and Chapman, 1977; Winner, 1979). The child may deliberately stretch the reference of a word in order to point out some perceived resemblance. The child who called the skywriting "scar" had in fact seen a scar on her mother and perhaps wanted to convey that the white line in the sky, with its adjacent dots, reminded her of the white line on her mother's body, with its adjacent stitch marks. Even Piaget, conservative in his assessment of young children's capacities, believed that unconventional word usage was sometimes based on pretense, and hence was nonliterally intended. Piaget went on to write, however, that such usages were verbalizations of "mere" images, momentary confusions which did not represent "true" concepts (1962, pp. 227–228). Nonetheless, because he accepted such usage as pretense, Piaget seems to have acknowledged that unconventional names are not necessarily indicative of a lexical error.

To distinguish unintentional misuses (as children are working out the meanings of words) from metaphoric uses (deliberate misuses once the meaning of a word has been worked out) is difficult because both are grounded in perceived similarity and both may appear highly inventive. But there is an important difference between the communicative functions of overextensions and metaphors. As mentioned above, overextensions fill lexical gaps, and once the gap is filled by the appropriate word, the overextension drops out. Metaphoric misuses do not usually fill gaps. Instead, the child typically misnames an object despite the fact that he possesses the appropriate name for it. He does so to point out a resemblance that has struck him as noteworthy. To count an utterance as a metaphor, then, we must have evidence that the child knows the appropriate, literal name for the metaphorically named object.

Distinguishing Metaphors from Anomalies and Overextensions

Although numerous researchers have admitted that early misuses of words might be metaphoric, there have been few attempts to distinguish metaphors from mistakes in a systematic manner. With this goal in mind, the spontaneous speech of one child was analyzed according to a set of criteria devised to distinguish metaphoric and nonmetaphoric word usage in early language (Winner, 1979). Evidence was also sought to determine whether there is a developmental order in the kinds of grounds and domains on which children's early metaphors (if they exist) are constructed. The child studied (Adam) was one of the children used by Brown (1973) in his longitudinal study of language acquisition. Adam's speech was recorded as he played with his mother and one of the experimenters at regular intervals from the time he was 2.3 to 4.10 years old.

In order to identify early metaphoric utterances and to exclude nonmetaphors, several steps were followed. First, words used in a manner not consonant with conventional adult usage were identified. These utterances were then subjected to further analysis to determine whether they were instances of mistakes (either overextensions or anomalous utterances) or metaphors. Utterances were considered *anomalies* if no basis for the name was apparent (as when Adam called a briefcase label "spaghetti"). Utterances were considered *overextensions* under either of the following conditions: (1) the word was used to apply to a set of similar referents (for example, when various kinds of stringlike objects were called "worm"); (2) there was no evidence that the child knew the literal name for the object named.

Utterances were considered *metaphors* if they satisfied one or more of the following conditions. (1) Either in prior use or immediately following the renaming, Adam called the renamed object by its literal name. For instance, he called a piece of string "my tail" and subsequently said that it was a piece of string. (2) An object was transformed through some kind of pretend gesture and was renamed according to what was suggested by the gesture. For instance, Adam held a horn like an eggbeater, made turning motions, and then announced "mixer." Such gestural transformations sometimes occurred abruptly, as Adam suddenly noted the transformational potentials of an object; at other times, they were motivated by a prior symbolic play sequence: a particular object was needed in symbolic play and an object in the vicinity was renamed accordingly.

If both of the above criteria were applicable, the case for metaphor was strong. But this rarely occurred. The first criterion is a stringent one because a record of Adam's total speech output was not available. And even if such a record existed, it would not have been sufficient, since Adam might have had a particular word in his lexicon without ever having produced it. Hence, the second criterion was considered adequate by itself, because the accompanying pretend gesture reveals that the object is being deliberately transformed. If one grants symbolic status to the object substitutions of symbolic play, then the accompanying renamings are certainly intended nonliterally. Whether the child knows the literal name of the renamed object is irrelevant here; all that matters is whether the child knows that the object is not what he is calling and using it as. And the evidence for this rests on the display of gestures in the pretend mode.

A third criterion was used in the absence of the two described above: the sheer probability that Adam knew the literal name of the renamed object. This assumption was made when the object in question was a highly familiar one. For example, Adam called two irons sitting on an ironing board "iron fish." There was no prior record in the transcripts of the use of the term "iron" to refer to irons. But by the age of three, Adam probably knew what an iron is and certainly knew the meaning of "fish." Thus, it would be implausible to insist that Adam intended the term "fish" literally.

The Emergence of Metaphor in Symbolic Play

Through the use of the criteria discussed above, the majority (79%) of Adam's unconventional utterances were shown to be deliberate nonliteral renamings. When the renamings failed to meet the criteria for metaphor, they were almost always overextensions rather than anomalies. During his 112 hours of recorded speech, Adam produced 185 utterances that satisfied the criteria for metaphor—averaging significantly more than one metaphor an hour. Almost all of the metaphors were of one sort: renamings (using nouns) of familiar physical objects. The predominance of metaphoric uses of nouns is consistent with the finding that the majority of the child's early vocabulary words are nouns (Clark, 1983). The metaphors could readily be categorized into two types: *symbolic play* metaphors, which grew out of pretend action transformations; and *sensory* metaphors, which arose out of a perceived physical similarity, without the support of pretense.

If Adam performed a pretend action on an object—treating it as if it were something else—and renamed it accordingly, the utterance was scored as a symbolic play metaphor. For instance, Adam tied tape around the stem of a microphone and said "microphone need a bib," and he put his foot inside a wastebasket and said "boot." In such cases the object was handled in a noncharacteristic way, and the action was necessary to the transformation. That is, the tape only became a bib as it was tied around a necklike object; the wastebasket only became a boot when his foot was placed inside it. These metaphors are similar to relational metaphors, discussed in the previous chapter, in that they are based on a functional and not a sensory similarity. Yet they are different from relational metaphors because the relationship is created, not discovered. Adam did not *perceive* a resemblance between the functions of two objects; rather, he perceived a potential for resemblance and then *created* the resemblance by engaging in some form of pretend action.

If Adam renamed an object without first transforming it through pretense, the metaphor was invariably based on some kind of physical similarity. The kind of physical similarity underlying these nonaction, sensory metaphors was almost always shape. This observation conflicts with the finding (based on older children) that action metaphors are easier to understand than those based on static grounds (Calhoun, 1984; Dent, 1984), but does conform to the finding that 80 to 90% of overextensions are based on shape and that in children's early vocabulary there are three to four times as many nouns as verbs (Clark, 1983). Hence, the type of similarity motivating early sensory metaphors is no different from that which motivates attempts at literal naming. (Symbolic play metaphors, by contrast, are based on dynamic, functional grounds—the actions and functions an object affords.) Examples of sensory metaphors include calling a red balloon attached to a green tube an "apple" on a "tree," calling the letter *J* a "cane," and calling a pencil a "big needle." (The child who identified the skywriting as a "scar" was also making a sensory metaphor.) Only rarely did children base metaphors on multiple sensory grounds (as in the apple example above, based on both shape and color). Usually shape alone served to ground the metaphor.

An analysis of the grounds underlying Adam's metaphors revealed that the type of metaphor he produced changed with age. At age two, Adam produced many more symbolic play than sensory metaphors (62% versus 25%). Hence, symbolic play was the condition for his first metaphors, and these metaphors were grounded on a functional similarity created through pretend action. By age four, the reverse pattern was found: most of Adam's metaphors were of the sensory (76%) rather than the symbolic play type (10%).

Thus, metaphors were found in Adam's speech when he was as young as age two, and these metaphors were elicited by resemblances perceived among the ordinary objects in his environment. These resemblances did not at first inhere solely in the objects themselves but were constructed out of the pretend actions of symbolic play. Although symbolic play metaphors may be based on sensory properties of the objects renamed, their critical feature is that the object is transformed on both a verbal and a gestural level. Adam's symbolic play metaphors declined sharply with development, giving way to a qualitatively different kind of metaphor, one based on sensory similarities alone. By age four, the majority of Adam's metaphors were based on the objects themselves, without the support of pretense.

To confirm the conclusions drawn from Adam's speech, longitudinal samples of the spontaneous speech of two other children were also studied (Winner, McCarthy, Kleinman, and Gardner, 1979). These children were subjects of a longitudinal study of symbolic development, including language development (Wolf and Gardner, in preparation). Detailed records of spontaneous utterances and their contexts were available. Although this second study lent support to the claim that symbolic play metaphors decline with age, a pattern of individual differences also emerged. The earliest metaphors of one of these children were always rooted in symbolic play. With age, this child began to produce some nonaction, sensory metaphors, but symbolic play metaphors remained the most common. The other child's earliest metaphors were equally divided between symbolic play and sensory types, and with age, symbolic play metaphors dropped out of her speech.

Thus, it appears that the two children engaged in very different styles of metaphor making. One paid scant attention to the properties of the objects renamed and used gesture to transform just about any object into anything else. He dipped a spoon into a blanket, lifted it to his mouth, and called the blanket "ice cream." He pretended to cut his mother's hair with a toy ladder and called the ladder "scissors." And he called a napkin that stuck to his hand a "puppet." For this child, the new pretend identity was primary, while the object that was transformed was secondary. What motivated the renaming was the desire to create a pretend object: to do so, he chose any available object and transformed it through pretense. In the other child's speech the properties of the object renamed were primary and in fact motivated the renaming. For an object to elicit a new name, it had to resemble its new identity. This child called long thin blocks "candles," a pillow whose corners resembled triangular ears a "cat," and a sewing machine whose side view resembled the bent head and neck of a horse a "table-horsey."

From these studies of early speech it appears that first metaphors arise either from the pretend action of symbolic play (yielding something different from an adult metaphor) or from the perception of sensory resemblances (yielding something closer to an adult metaphor). Classification by sensory and functional similarity are the child's two primary means of organizing reality (Clark, 1973; Nelson, 1974), and these are the modes by which children construct their first metaphors. The metaphors of any individual child are likely with age to become grounded less often in pretend function and more often in sensory similarity. The dominance of one or the other of these modes, however, may reflect individual differences in styles of early metaphor.

The Relation of Early Metaphor to Adult Metaphor

Even if we concur that some early renamings are in fact deliberate metaphors, we still need to determine whether these metaphors have the asymmetrical topic-vehicle structure of adult, "mature" metaphors. There are two issues to consider here. First, does the direction of the child's metaphors go from vehicle to topic (as in an adult metaphor) or from topic to vehicle? That is, is the vehicle used to reveal something new about the topic, or is the topic simply a tool for imagining the vehicle? Second, do early metaphors show the kind of asymmetry that differentiates metaphoric from literal similarity, in which topic and vehicle share properties of high salience to the vehicle and low salience to the topic?

Directionality. A cogent case has been made by Marjanovic (1983) that symbolic play metaphors are less fully metaphoric than sensory ones because they lack the directionality of adult metaphors. In a mature metaphor the vehicle serves to direct our attention to the topic: hence, the topic is the focus of the metaphor. When Hamlet calls the world an "unweeded garden," we adjust our understanding of "world," not "garden." In symbolic play metaphors the situation is reversed; the topic is a way of materializing an imagined object: hence the vehicle is the focus of the metaphor. When the child called the ladder "scissors," he was not suggesting that ladders be seen in a new way, because the ladder was not important, and many objects could have served the same function. The child was simply using the ladder to stand for an imaginary scissors. Contrast this to the other child's use of "table-horsey" to refer to a sewing machine. Here, the focus of the metaphor is, as in Hamlet's, the topic (sewing machine). The vehicle (table-horsey) plays the role of refocusing our attention on the sewing machine so that it will be seen in a new way. This analysis of symbolic play metaphors is convincing and suggests that such metaphors lack the asymmetry of full-blown metaphors.

Salience imbalance. It is possible that preschoolers are able to produce names based on similarity without differentiating between literal and nonliteral similarity (Ortony, 1979a). As argued in Chapter 3, cases of literal similarity involve matches between elements of the same conventional category that share properties highly salient to both (for example, lakes are like oceans, since they share the salient property of containing large amounts of water). In contrast, cases of nonliteral similarity involve links between elements from different categories that share properties more salient to the vehicle than to the topic (for example, fields are like oceans since they are both characterized by great size and wavelike motion; these shared properties are, however, more salient to oceans than to hayfields and hence cause us to look anew at hayfields.

We cannot assume that a child's deliberate renamings are based on this kind of salience imbalance. For instance, even though Adam may have known that a pencil was not really a needle, he may have believed that both pencils and needles belonged to the same category and that thinness and sharpness were properties of equal salience to pencils and needles. Hence, when he called the pencil a big needle, he may have been naming on the basis of literal rather than metaphoric similarity. To determine whether preschool children discriminate between literal and metaphoric similarity, one needs to intervene experimentally.

To demonstrate that children can distinguish between literal and nonliteral similarity, Mendelsohn and colleagues (1984) presented four-year-olds with alternative modes of categorization and noted whether a preference for conventional or metaphoric classification was shown. If children were to show that their primary mode of classification was conventional, this would provide support for the claim that their apparent metaphors at least involved an *overriding* of a conventional category boundary and hence were different from literal classifications. The paradigm used was a sorting task consisting of triads of pictures, words, or a combination. In the mixed pictorial-verbal condition, for instance, there was a target picture (such as a red lollipop) along with two verbally presented choices ("chocolate bar," and "stop sign"). The experimenter showed the child the target picture and then read the two verbal choices and asked, "Which would you pick for this?" (referring to the picture). If children selected "chocolate bar," the match was considered conventional and within-category (both are candy): if they selected "stop sign," the match was considered unconventional and based on visual similarity (both are red and round but belong to different domains). Conventional matches outnumbered visual ones. Four-year-olds thus discriminated between literal and nonliteral similarity, and their conventional categories were the same as those of adults. Hence, when four-year-olds produce unconventional names for objects based on similarity, such utterances must be considered deliberate overridings of conventional category boundaries.

Another study probing children's ability to differentiate literal and metaphoric similarity has suggested that the distinction is made by four-year-olds but not by three-year-olds (Vosniadou and Ortony, 1983a). In this study children were given two tasks. First, in a *comparison* task, children heard sentences such as "A river is like a ———" and were given two possible endings to choose from. The ending pairs were of three types: (1) literal/metaphor (for "river," the choice was between "lake" [literal] and "snake" [metaphor]); (2) literal/anomaly ("lake" versus "cat"); (3) metaphor/anomaly ("snake" versus "cat"). On this task either metaphoric or literal choices would be correct. If children chose more of either of these than of the anomalous choices, they would demonstrate that they could distinguish anomaly from meaningful similarity. Second, in a *categorization* task, the items were rephrased in the form "A river is the same sort of thing as ———," and there were two types of ending pairs: literal/metaphor and literal/anomaly. Here the literal choice was clearly correct, the metaphoric and anomalous clearly wrong.

The subjects were three- through six-year-olds, and adults. The pairs of terms used in the tasks were taken from sensory metaphors that have been reported in the language of young children by writers such as Chukovsky, 1968, and Koch, 1970. Three-year-olds proved able to distinguish anomalous from meaningful similarity, as demonstrated by their rejection of the anomalies on the comparison task. But they failed to distinguish between metaphoric and literal similarity. This was shown by their being equally likely to select the metaphoric choices on the comparison and categorization tasks. Thus, they were just as likely to say that "A river is the same kind of thing as a snake" as they were "A river is like a snake." In striking contrast, children just one year older selected the literal choices on the categorization task. On the comparison task neither the literal nor the metaphoric choices were preferred, and this was true of all ages tested.

Although three-year-olds were able, overall, to reject the anomalies, their grasp of the distinction between an anomalous and a meaningful ending was tenuous. On some items they consistently chose the anomalous choice. For instance, given the sentence "Eyes are like ———" and the choice "bicycles/ ears," they often selected bicycles, perhaps because bicycle wheels are round like eyes. In this case physical attributes (such as circularity) may have proved more important to three-year-olds than conventional category membership (facial features). This interpretation is similar to that reached by Wagner and associates (1982), who found that for infants abstract, amodal similarities were more prepotent than similarities between stimuli in the same sensory modality (see Chapter 4).

Thus, three- and four-year-olds appear to perform quite differently on this task. Three-year-olds perceive only an undifferentiated type of similarity (one which they do not even consistently distinguish from anomaly), whereas four-year-olds distinguish between metaphoric and literal similarity, as indicated by their ability to reject the metaphoric choice on the categorization task.

The types of metaphors used by both Mendelsohn and associates (1984) and Vosniadou and Ortony (1983a) were sensory ones. Hence these findings bear only on utterances that might be considered sensory metaphors, and not on apparent metaphors grounded in pretend action. The results of Vosniadou and Ortony's study suggest that perhaps the apparent sensory metaphors of a two- and three-year-old should be viewed differently from those of a four-year-old. In light of this study the sensory metaphors produced by Adam at age two, for instance, might be based on undifferentiated similarity rather than on a recognition of metaphoric similarity. To be sure, he knew that he was using a name that did not literally apply (as indicated by vocabulary evidence). But this assessment does not distinguish a deliberate renaming based on literal as opposed to metaphoric similarity.

Although children's first metaphors may lack the kind of salience imbalance we find in an adult metaphor, it is risky to draw strong conclusions about metaphors created spontaneously and in context on the basis of what children do with metaphors they are given and asked to judge. Vosniadou and Ortony's results depend on the child's ability to differentiate linguistically between "the same sort of thing as" and "is like." If children are insensitive to the subtle distinction in meaning between these two phrases, they fail the task. They might be insensitive to the linguistic coding of this distinction yet still be sensitive to the distinction between a link based on literal versus metaphoric similarity. The problem, of course, is how to tap such sensitivity without relying on metalinguistic measures.

Other differences. Children's early metaphors differ from adult metaphors in other ways besides lack of topic-vehicle directionality and salience imbalance. Most important, early metaphors are usually based on sensory similarity or pretend actions. Nonsensory metaphors other than those based on pretend actions are rare. Sensory properties are very salient to young children, and they may know little else about objects. Vosniadou and Ortony (1983a) point out, for instance, that adults, in contrast to children, know a great deal more about the sun than its shape and color. They are aware of its function, its position in the solar system, as well as many of the associations it has come to take on (life, energy, passion). Thus, adult metaphors are likely to be based on properties besides (or as well as) sensory ones. As discussed in the previous chapter, children are more likely to understand sensory than nonsensory metaphors for this very same reason: children simply know less about the functions than the appearances of things, because the former depends on learning and experience whereas the latter depends only on direct perception.

From Metaphor to Analogy

The incidence of spontaneous metaphoric speech appears to decline rather dramatically during the early school years. This has been noted in several observational studies (Billow, 1981; Marti, 1979; Snyder, 1979). Billow (1981) recorded all apparent metaphors spoken by children between the ages of two and six; utterances were scored as metaphoric if the scorers could see a similarity between the name given and the referent. The number of observations containing one or more metaphors decreased sharply with age: among children between the ages of 2.7 and 3.6, 50% of the observations contained one or more metaphors; between 3.7 and 4.6, the figure was 39%; between 4.7 and 5.6, 33%; and between 5.7 and 6.0, 20%.

One reason for the decline in metaphor use is that the kinds of activities yielding metaphors decline with age. For instance, when a child built a sand castle and called it a "castle," Billow scored this as metaphor; and symbolic play renamings—such as scooping up water and calling it "ice cream"—were also scored as metaphors. If such constructive and symbolic play declines with age, then metaphor (so-defined) will also decline. I do not think, however, that we can attribute the decline in metaphor production entirely to the decline in metaphor-stimulating activities. Other observers have also noted the decline with age, which occurs for all types of metaphors (Marti, 1979; Snyder, 1979). Moreover, a resistance to metaphor has often been noted anecdotally in children of elementary school age. Children around the ages of eight, nine, and ten often reject metaphors addressed to them, insisting, for instance, that colors cannot be loud, and people cannot be icy (Gardner et al., 1975).

A conversation I had recently makes the point nicely. Recall the preschool child (mentioned at the beginning of this chapter) who, when suffering from a stomach ache, announced that she had a "fire engine" in her stomach. Several years later, I told her what she had said and asked her what it meant. She did not know. I then asked her whether it would make more sense for someone with a stomach ache to say that he had a fire engine or a pillow in his stomach. She responded very definitely. It would be "wrong," she explained, to say "fire engine," because a fire engine would not fit in a stomach; it would be better to say "pillow" because this would fit! Because of the resistance to the use of metaphor during the elementary school years, this period has been called the *literal* or *conventional* stage (Winner, 1982). Manifestations of this concern with convention can be found not only in the domain of language but also in children's drawings (Gardner, 1980; Gardner and Winner, 1982).

Children not only stop producing metaphors, they also lose interest in metaphoric constructions altogether. This was demonstrated by Gardner and colleagues in a study (1975) in which children as young as age three had to choose one of several endings to sentences such as "He looks as gigantic as . . ." and "His voice was as quiet as . . ." One of the endings resulted in a novel simile ("as gigantic as a double-decker ice cream cone in a baby's hand," "as quiet as dawn in a ghost town"), one in a trite simile ("as gigantic as a skyscraper in the center of town," "as quiet as a mouse sitting in a room"), one in an anomaly ("as gigantic as a clock from a department store"), and one in a literal comparison in which no category boundary was crossed ("as gigantic as the most gigantic person in the whole world," "as quiet as the quietest sound we've heard"). Children also had to produce an ending of their own.

On the selection task preschoolers chose at random. Seven-year-olds preferred the literal endings, apparently because these comparisons (as constructed here) expressed the adjective (gigantic, quiet) in its most extreme instantiation. "I didn't choose 'as boiling as a teapot whistling' because that's less boiling than 'the most boiling thing in the world,' " one typical subject explained. Children of this age rejected the novel endings: "a double-decker cone can't be gigantic because I'm taller than a cone," one said. Eleven-year-olds preferred trite endings. They rejected the literal comparisons because they "didn't say anything new." They also often rejected the novel endings, as did the seven-year-olds, insisting for instance that a color cannot be loud. Preference for trite endings declined somewhat after age eleven, as preference for novel endings increased. Adolescents preferred trite and novel endings equally. It was only the adults who preferred the novel to the conventional endings, and even their preference was not very strong (53% to 47%).

On the production task the most common responses in all age groups were those classified as conventional. Preschoolers, however, produced a higher percentage of novel endings than did children aged seven, eleven, and fourteen. Indeed, preschoolers produced as high a proportion of novel endings as did adults. Novel endings by preschoolers included "weather as boiling as your head popping open," "quiet as a magic marker," and "sad as a pimple." Preschoolers also produced more than three times as many inappropriate (anomalous) endings—such as "tall as an Indian"—as did older age groups. Although all ages produced many more trite endings than any other kind, a change was noted with age: whereas seven-year-olds produced rather bare trite endings ("as soft as a pillow"; "as strong as a rock"), eleven-year-olds and adults produced embellished trite endings: for instance, "as strong as a gigantic boulder sticking in the ground," or "as light as the pastel colors in Van Gogh." Despite some of the interesting elaborations, these endings were still considered trite, since the core comparison was ordinary and not one that aligned elements infrequently compared. This study provides evidence that preschool children are more apt to produce metaphoric comparisons than are elementary school children, who seem to resist metaphoric language and to prefer literal or conventional uses of words.

When this same task was administered by Pollio and Pickens (1980), the decline in trite selections after age eleven, reported by Gardner and his colleagues (1975), was not found; nor was the equal popularity (by the time of adolescence) of trite and novel selections. Instead, Pollio and Pickens found that preference for both trite and novel comparisons increased with age, but trite comparisons were preferred at all ages. In their study the oldest subjects were aged sixteen, whereas in the earlier study (Gardner et al., 1975) the oldest were aged nineteen. Pickens and Pollio (1979) administered the same task to college age subjects, and found that these older subjects also showed a preference for trite over novel comparisons. As Pollio and Pickens (1980) point out, the task demands of this study are high, and children may well think that the best answer is the safest one. The trite comparisons were familiar and hence may well have appeared more likely to be "right." Without further research, there is no obvious way to explain the discrepancy between the results of the Gardner and Pollio studies, except to speculate that the subjects in the former may—for whatever reason—have been more willing to be "creative."

Have children at the literal stage lost the competence for metaphor, or has it simply gone "underground"? There is considerable evidence that the capacity is not lost, and that what we are witnessing has to do with performance and preference, not underlying ability. The likelihood of producing a metaphor at this age seems to depend on the type of task used to elicit it. For instance, on a school-type task (writing a composition on an imaginative topic), elementary school children produce few metaphors, either novel or trite. On a comparison task, however, in which children are asked to come up with as many similarities as possible for pairs of words (such as "clock and child," "can and box"), novel responses actually increase with age, at least from fourth to fifth grades (Pollio and Pollio, 1974). Further evidence that the capacity to produce metaphor is not lost comes from a training study in which ten-year-olds were taught (over the course of eight weeks) to produce novel similes (Silverman et al., 1975). (See also Pollio, 1973, for another training study demonstrating that elementary school children can be taught to produce novel metaphoric comparisons.)

Although the incidence of metaphoric renamings appears to decline during the early school years, the invention of analogies may increase. Anecdotal reports suggest that the playful renamings of the preschool years give way to extended analogies used in the service of understanding. Preschoolers seem to delight in metaphoric renamings. Metaphors grow out of symbolic play and appear to serve a playful function. To be sure, they help the child make sense of the universe (since they are a form of classification, and hence of ordering); but they are affectively tinged with playfulness, humor, and delight. In contrast, older children seem more serious about how they use words. Although they are less willing to play with words, they seem more willing to work out extended analogies (based on the same types of grounds as metaphors) in order to help clarify a novel concept for themselves. For instance, a six-year-old who was trying to understand the concept of medical "side effects" asked her mother if side effects were like using a scissors to open a can and bending the scissors in the process (D. Wolf, personal communication). Here, both topic and vehicle are stated, the ground is explicitly stated, and the ground is relational rather than sensory. A similar example, but one based on more sensory similarity, was provided by a ten-year-old. Seated at our dinner table with a messy one-year-old who was spilling food all over the table, the older child explained that it did not make sense to wipe the table until the baby had finished eating. He compared this to the futility of washing one's hands while working with glue. It makes no sense to clean up until one is completely finished, he said, since your hands just keep getting sticky all over again. This analogy arose in the course of explanation and understanding, and its function seemed to be more to clarify than to delight in a similarity perceived. In both these examples the children were *using* perceived similarity for purposes of explanation, rather than simply *pointing out* perceived similarity.

Mendelsohn, Winner, and Gardner (1980) carried out a study to investigate the following hypothesis: at the age at which spontaneous metaphors decline, the production of analogies in the service of understanding and explanation increases. Children between the ages of seven and eleven were asked to explain various concepts to a puppet who was said to be from Neptune and ignorant about life on Earth. For example, children had to explain how a radio works, what it means to tell a secret, and what it means to retire. On half of the items children were simply asked to tell the puppet "what this is like." On the other half children were also given a specific domain with which to compare the concept to be explained (for example, "Can you think of anything to do with clothing that is like retiring?").

The ability to produce analogies increased steadily with age when a domain probe was used. The ability to produce analogies with no specific domain probe also increased with age, particularly from ages nine to eleven (the "prime" years of the literal stage). The domain probe hindered the youngest children (they performed best with no probe), helped the nine-year-olds, and had no effect on the eleven-year-olds. Without a domain probe, the nine-year-olds produced rather mundane analogies. For instance, asked to explain the concept of a flower wilting and given no domain of comparison, one nine-year-old said that just as a person needs water for his body, a flower needs water for its stem. Contrast this to an eleven-year-old's response when given no probe: this child said that a flower needs vitamins and minerals from dirt just like a car needs gas; vitamins and minerals from dirt make the flower "go" just like gas makes a car go. The eleven-year-old's response is more "stretched" than that of the nine-year-old. The responses of the seven-year-olds also displayed this quality of tension, or stretch: one seven-year-old said that tree roots are like wires because "wires store electricity and let electricity run through them, just like roots which let rain water run through them." Thus, the seven-year-olds' responses were in some sense more similar to those of the eleven-year-olds than to those of the nine-year-olds.

This study demonstrates that the ability to produce extended analogies in the service of explanation increases with age. During the literal stage, when children resist making metaphors, they do not resist constructing analogies. Yet the literal stage still makes itself felt: nine-year-olds tend to make rather safe comparisons, unlike both older and younger children. That they have the capacity to produce more original ones is demonstrated by their improved performance with the domain probes. What is noteworthy, in my view, is that even on a straightforward scientific analogy task, the effects of the literal stage are evident. Recall that the child who compared side effects to bending a scissors while opening a can was only aged six, whereas the child who made the far safer analogy of comparing wiping a table with washing one's hands after using glue was aged ten and thus in the midst of the literal years.

Studies of children's ability to create metaphors in language confirm the view developed in Chapter 4 that metaphoric ability is present in the preschool years. Within a year or two after children begin to name objects, they show the capacity to extend words deliberately on the basis of metaphoric similarity. These similarities are not only sensory but also relational, in the case of symbolic play metaphors. Because children are initially insensitive to the topic-vehicle structure, these metaphors work in the wrong direction: the topic is used to support the vehicle, the vehicle reveals nothing new or unexpected about the topic, and any number of topics could have been used to support the imagined vehicle. Moreover, there is no good evidence that children's first metaphors are based on nonliteral similarity with salience imbalance, and it appears that children do not at first differentiate literal and nonliteral similarity. This finding suggests that when preschool children appear to comprehend metaphors, they understand them as based on literal rather than metaphoric similarity. In other words, they do not sense that a metaphoric match involves a greater "stretch" than a literal one.

Taken together, the evidence suggests that the comprehension and production of metaphor develop along the same track. What is present as early as can be assessed is the ability to perceive similarities, both sensory and nonsensory; what develops in each case is sensitivity to topic-vehicle structure. Although the latter is important to metaphor, it is clearly not as critical to the *core* of metaphoric ability as is sensitivity to the kinds of similarities on which metaphors are based. Without sensitivity to topic-vehicle structure, at least partial understanding is possible. Without sensitivity to grounds, no understanding is possible.

Chapter 6

Metaphor and Cognition

So far we have ignored the question of the relation of metaphoric ability to other cognitive and linguistic skills. Since metaphor comprehension appears to be constrained by familiarity with the domains involved, one would expect it to be unaffected by cognitive level. But given the early emergence of metaphors in speech, and their prevalence, one would expect metaphors to serve more than a trivial, ornamental function. They should be used for a reason. Also, given the prevalence of metaphors in ordinary language and the ease with which they are usually understood, one would expect metaphors to be processed as directly as literal language; special inferential processes for metaphor comprehension ought to be necessary only for special cases. These expectations are explored in this final chapter on metaphor.

The Role of Logical Abilities

It has been argued that metaphor comprehension is related to the kinds of logical classification abilities identified by Inhelder and Piaget (1964) as emerging in middle and late childhood (Billow, 1975; Cometa and Eson, 1978). These abilities have been seen as prerequisite cognitive structures for metaphor comprehension. Billow (1975) examined the comprehension of two types of metaphor—those based on sensory similarity (called "similarity metaphors" in this study), and those based on relational similarity (called "proportional metaphors"). In a similarity metaphor, such as "The butterfly is a rainbow," the two terms are classified together on the basis of the visual similarity between them—both are multicolored. In contrast, a proportional metaphor, such as "My head is an apple without any core," is based on four terms linked to each other relationally (head is to brain as apple is to core); the similarity between the relation of head to brain and the relation of apple to core provides the basis for the comparison.

Billow sought to demonstrate that comprehension of similarity metaphors depends on an understanding of class inclusion, that is, recognizing an object as belonging to several levels of classes: that a tulip, for example, can be a member of both the superordinate class of flowers and the subclass of tulips. Billow reasoned that in order to understand a metaphor such as "The butterfly is a rainbow," the child must recognize that both topic and vehicle belong to the superordinate class of multicolored objects. According to Inhelder and Piaget (1964), an understanding of class inclusion relationships emerges only after six or seven years of age, when the child enters the stage of concrete operations. Comprehension of proportional metaphors, Billow hypothesized, emerges only at adolescence during the stage of formal operations, the stage at which Inhelder and Piaget (1958) found evidence for the emergence of an understanding of proportionality.

By examining the relation between performance on the metaphor and logical reasoning tasks, Billow tested the hypothesis that similarity metaphor comprehension depends on concrete operational skill, while proportional metaphor comprehension depends on formal operational skill. He gave children between the ages of five and thirteen similarity and proportional metaphors to paraphrase and also asked them to perform class inclusion tasks (to assess concrete operational skills) and combinatorial reasoning tasks (to assess formal operational skills). He found that half of the children were able to understand the similarity metaphors but were not able to perform the class inclusion task. In contrast, understanding of the proportional metaphors was highly correlated with performance on the formal operational test of combinatorial reasoning. Billow concluded that concrete operations are not necessary in order to understand similarity metaphors (hence, similarity metaphor comprehension is an early skill), but that formal operations are necessary in order to understand proportional metaphors (and hence, proportional metaphor comprehension is a late skill).

Adopting the same kind of approach but using different Piagetian tasks, Cometa and Eson (1978) tested the hypothesis that metaphor comprehension depends not on class inclusion but rather on class intersection—that is, finding the intersection between two classes which at first may appear not to intersect at all. In a metaphor such as "Everyone says that the man is a sheep," the listener must align two classes that at first appear to be incongruous. To understand this metaphor, he must construct the intersection of the two classes "man" and "sheep." According to Inhelder and Piaget (1964), understanding of class intersection is a late development because the child must focus only on a subset of each class. In contrast to metaphors, literal sentences such as "The animal is a sheep" are based on class inclusion relationships. Thus, Cometa and Eson argued that Billow focused on a logical operation which should have no relation to metaphor.

Cometa and Eson constructed a small set of metaphors including "My thoughts are twisted when I wake up" and "When the wind blew, the leaves began to dance." Children between the ages of five and thirteen were asked both to paraphrase the metaphors and to explain their paraphrases—for example, to explain why we use the term "twisted" to mean "confused." To test the hypothesized relationship between metaphor comprehension and class intersection, Cometa and Eson also administered several of Piaget's tasks: a test of conservation of amount (to determine whether children understand that the quantity of liquid in a glass is unaffected by being transferred into a glass of another size—indicative of concrete operational skill), a test of class intersection (a late concrete operational skill), and a test of combinatorial reasoning in which children have to combine chemicals systematically in order to discover which combination produces a desired result (a formal operational skill).

In one of the intersection tasks, children saw a picture of a row of green objects (an umbrella, a fish, a book, and a butterfly, all green). Perpendicular to this row was a row of leaves of different colors, none green. At the corner at which the two rows met, there was an empty cell. The task was to fill in the cell, in this case with a green leaf—the object that forms the intersection of the class of green objects and the class of leaves.

The ability to paraphrase metaphors was found only among children demonstrating concrete operational thought (as measured by conservation of amount). This finding was not due to age differences, as was determined when nonconservers were compared to a group of conservers of the same age and only the conservers paraphrased successfully. Whereas conservation was related to paraphrase ability, success on the class intersection task was not. But the ability to *explain* paraphrases was found only among children who could perform class intersection. Although some understood the principle of class intersection but could not give explanations, no child who gave adequate explanations failed the class intersection task. Formal operational logic (as measured by the chemicals task) proved unrelated to the ability to explain and paraphrase.

Some illustrations may prove useful. Here is an example of responses by two children, one of whom failed the intersection task and one of whom solved it. Aged 7.2 years, the child who failed the task offered an adequate paraphrase for "When the wind blew, the leaves began to dance": "They move all around and go back and forth." But this child was incapable of explaining why "dance" means "move around." She said, "Well, I don't know. People are not the same as leaves. People have eyes and mouths and leaves don't really dance. They don't have feet!" Contrast this to a child aged 10.2 who solved the intersection task. The explanation given for "dance" (after a successful paraphrase) was "It describes it pretty good. 'Cause people shake back and forth when they dance, so it's just like the leaves do when the wind pushes them." Cometa and Eson drew three conclusions from this study: the logic of early concrete operations is required to paraphrase metaphor; the logic of class intersection is required to explain paraphrases; and formal operational logic is unrelated to metaphor comprehension.

Although the studies by Billow, and Cometa and Eson, were reasonable first attempts to investigate the relationship between metaphor understanding and Piagetian stages, their conclusions can be challenged on both methodological and theoretical grounds. In an investigation of the relationship between a Piagetian stage and a particular ability, one can get just about any result one wants by slightly altering the tasks (see Vosniadou, 1987). Moreover, the entire concept of Piagetian stages has been called into question by findings showing substantial lags in age of acquisition on tasks purported to measure skills in the same stage (Gelman and Baillargeon, 1983). If stages have not held up, it makes little sense to ask whether there is a relationship between a metaphoric ability and a Piagetian stage. Although one might argue that it is still possible to determine whether metaphor comprehension is related to performance on a particular Piagetian task such as class inclusion or class intersection, rather than to a general stage, the fact of task variability must be accounted for. High variability on the same task has been found such that when the wording is changed, or a verbal task is changed into a nonverbal one, performance is radically altered.

The same problem holds for metaphor. As argued in Chapter 3, the type of measure used dramatically affects how successful comprehension of metaphor is revealed. Both Billow, and Cometa and Eson, used a difficult measure—paraphrase—to assess metaphor comprehension. Had they used nonverbal measures they might have found earlier comprehension. The type of metaphor also constrains comprehension, as was discussed in Chapter 4. Billow's similarity metaphors were sensory (butterfly = rainbow), whereas two out of seven of Cometa and Eson's metaphors were relational ("My thoughts are twisted when I wake up"; "He couldn't pay attention because his mind was cloudy"). As Vosniadou (1987) points out, since Billow used verbal classification tasks and simple metaphors, he was able to show that similarity metaphors were understood before children could succeed on a class inclusion task. Had he used nonverbal classification tasks and similarity metaphors based on conceptual resemblance, he would undoubtedly have found the reverse. Cometa and Eson used nonverbal Piagetian tasks but more difficult metaphors than Billow, and hence found that an understanding of the logic of class intersection preceded metaphor comprehension. In brief, given that there is no pure measure of metaphor comprehension, and given the questionable status of Piagetian stages, investigations of the relationship between metaphor comprehension and Piagetian stage are, in my view, limited. The most one can conclude from such studies is whether there is a relationship between a particular logical task presented in a particular way and a particular type of metaphor.

Other attempts to discover a link between metaphor comprehension and different kinds of skills and sensitivities have also yielded few strong claims. Kogan and colleagues (1980) carried out a series of studies to investigate whether metaphoric sensitivity was related to intellectual aptitude and achievement, divergent thinking, physiognomic perception (such as grouping certain kinds of colors with certain line patterns), and teachers' ratings on a variety of intellectual, affective, and behavioral measures. These studies demonstrated only a few correlations. There was no clear relationship between verbal intelligence (as measured by standardized tests) and sensitivity to metaphor. It was found that metaphor scores do correlate with divergent thinking, physiognomic perception, and aesthetic sensitivity— but possibly only if such sensitivity is assessed by art teachers. It is interesting to note that metaphoric sensitivity seems to be unrelated to other forms of intelligence and most highly related to skills which appear to overlap with metaphor, such as physiognomic and aesthetic sensitivity. It may even be unrelated to verbal intelligence of the kind ordinarily valued in schools and assessed by standardized tests.

Metaphors as Cognitive Tools

Creative scientists often report that their most inventive ideas were the result of applying an observation about one domain to a very different domain, by analogy. The planetary model of the atom, the hydraulic model of the circulatory system, and the computer model of the brain are all models based on analogies (Boden, 1977). These kinds of metaphoric models are not just a clever way of making one's discovery clear to others; rather, if we are to believe the reports of creative scientists, they are integral to the process of discovery.

The evidence suggests that the functions served by metaphor are primarily cognitive ones, in contrast to those served by irony which, I contend, are primarily social. We choose a metaphor over a literal description for several reasons: metaphors are economical, vivid, and memorable, and sometimes they are the only way we have to say what we want to say (Ortony, 1975). The effect of a metaphor is to clarify, to explain, to reveal—to alter the listener's understanding of the topic. Metaphor helps us to acquire knowledge about new domains, and also has the effect of restructuring our organization of knowledge.

• Acquiring New Knowledge

In Thomas Edison's first attempt at creating the kinetoscope, an early motion picture machine, he used a cylinder covered with a spiral of images. The cylinder rotated continuously while the viewer looked through an eye piece at the images. This created the illusion of a motion picture. The idea for this device can be traced to his invention of ten years earlier—the phonograph, which also has a rotating cylinder with spirals (in this case, sound grooves). The phonograph cylinder also came with an instrument through which the perceiver deciphered the spirals—a stylus (Broad, 1985). Thus, the idea for the motion picture was derived by analogy from a very different kind of instrument, one which produced sound, not images.

This is but one of many examples of scientific discoveries in which metaphoric (sometimes called "analogical") thinking plays a critical role. The perception of a similarity never seen before may lead nowhere, or it may lead to discovery. The perception of novel similarities—similarities across widely divergent domains (sound and picture)—is no different from the kind of similarity perception that underlies the understanding and construction of novel metaphors.

Metaphoric thinking is important in ordinary cognitive tasks as well as in scientific discovery. It may well be the primary route by which we acquire new information. There is evidence that in reasoning we do not use content-free, general inference rules that apply across domains (Rumelhart and Norman, 1981; Wason and Johnson-Laird, 1972); rather, we think about a new domain by reasoning analogically from what we know about a familiar domain.

There is empirical evidence that metaphoric thinking enables adults to acquire knowledge about new domains (Gick and Holyoak, 1980; Hayes and Tierney, 1982; Schustack and Anderson, 1979). Gick and Holyoak investigated the role of analogical thinking in achieving a solution to Duncker's (1945) radiation problem. In this well-known problem the subject must figure out how to irradiate a tumor so that the tumor receives enough rays for it to be destroyed, without harming the surrounding healthy tissue. The difficulty is that the dosage necessary to destroy the tumor is also sufficient to destroy healthy tissue.

To investigate the role of analogy in solving this problem, researchers devised a problem and solution in a domain different from the medical domain. They presented some subjects, for instance, with a story about a general who wants to capture a fortress in the center of a country. Roads, which radiate outward from the fortress, are mined and will be blown up if a large troop of soldiers passes by. Thus, a full-scale attack along one road is impossible. The solution reached by the general is to divide the soldiers into groups and send each group on a different road so that they converge simultaneously on the fortress. An analogous solution to the radiation problem is to send low intensity radiation to the tumor from many different directions. When the rays converge at the tumor, there will be sufficient intensity to destroy the tumor. This is a sensible solution, but one which most subjects do not think of spontaneously (Duncker, 1945).

These two problems are structurally similar: both involve an object to be conquered (tumor, fortress), and objects (healthy tissue, soldiers) that must be spared. And the solution offered in the military problem suggests an analogous solution in the medical problem. The radiation problem is just the sort of ill-defined problem—without an obvious answer—for which an analogy from a different domain might trigger a solution. To benefit from the military example, the subject must form a representation of the military problem and map this onto the radiation problem. Given the remoteness of the two domains (military and medical), the mappings can only be relational: for example, the subject might notice that in each case the object to be conquered is in the center of something. To generate a parallel solution to the radiation problem, the subject must map "army" onto "radiation," and "fortress" onto "tumor," and then apply the concept of dividing and converging troops.

Subjects first read one of three military stories, each suggesting a different analogous solution to the radiation problem. They then read the radiation problem and were told to talk out loud while trying to solve it; they were also given a hint: they were told to use the first story in order to solve the radiation problem. Overwhelmingly, subjects generated solutions that were analogous to the military story. For example, all ten subjects who heard the story about the general produced the analogous solution; not one control subject (who heard no military story) did so. An analysis of the problem-solving protocols (what subjects said as they tried to find a solution) suggested that analogous solutions were generated through a conscious process of mapping correspondences between the two stories. Some subjects mapped the stories in great detail; others needed to see only one or two points of correspondence in order to generate the analogous solution. When no hint was provided, however, subjects failed to generate the analogous solution. This study is an experimental simulation of the kind of analogical thinking that has been reported to occur in creative problem solving. The fact that the hint was necessary suggests that one of the major blocks to the use of metaphoric thinking in problem solving is not an *inability* to perceive a similarity between domains, but a failure to notice the similarity *spontaneously*.

When children understand metaphors, they are able to put them to the same uses as adults, as has been demonstrated in several studies: children can benefit from both explicit and implicit analogies, and also from metaphoric uses of language. The benefit takes the form of both superior recall and comprehension. For example, Vosniadou and Ortony (1983b) gave six- and eight-year-olds two kinds of texts to read. One group received texts with analogies (the functioning of white blood cells in the body was described by explicit analogy to soldiers) and the other group received texts about the same subject but without analogies. The children were then questioned about their understanding of the texts and were tested on their recall. Children who had read texts with analogies performed better on both tasks. Interestingly, children seemed to know which properties from the analogized domain to transfer to the topic domain. That is, they realized that if white blood cells are like soldiers, they function to protect; they did not make the inference that the cells wear uniforms (transfer of a physical property) or that they use guns (transfer of a physical activity). Instead, for the most part they transferred general functions—just those kinds of abstract, nonsensory properties that lie at the heart of conceptual metaphors. There was, however, one kind of transfer error that children could not resist: they attributed human emotions to inanimate objects. The white blood cells, for instance, were described as "brave." But children used such anthropomorphic descriptions whether or not they read the text with analogies. This tendency may reflect either a lack of distinction between human and nonhuman objects or, more likely, an idiomatic way of talking that children do not intend literally.

The finding that children did not transfer human properties

to cells at the physical level shows that the distinction between human and nonhuman is present to at least some extent. This conflicts with Keil's (1979) claim, discussed above, that children under the age of eleven have not worked out the distinctions between the human, animal, and plant domains. If these distinctions were not present, we could not account for the absence of physical transfer errors in Vosniadou and Ortony's study. The discrepancy in findings may be due to the fact that Keil's measure called upon metalinguistic skills (reflecting on whether plants can be "sorry," for example) and hence is likely to under-represent children's knowledge.

Whereas Vosniadou and Ortony showed that children can benefit from explicit analogies, Holyoak, Junn, and Billman (1984) found that children (including preschoolers) can make use of a nonexplicit analogy to solve a problem. They tested preschool children and ten- and eleven-year-olds by seating them in front of two bowls on a table, one within reach, one out of reach. One bowl contained gumballs, the other was empty. And on the table were various objects: a cane, a sheet of heavy paper, a hollow cardboard tube, scissors, string, tape, paper clips, and rubber bands. The children were asked to figure out as many ways as possible of transferring the balls from the full to the empty bowl without leaving their seats.

Before being asked to solve the problem, half of the children heard one of two stories that contained a problem analogous to the one that they would later be asked to solve, and a solution analogous to one that would solve their problem. But the analogies were not pointed out to the children. In the "magic staff" group children heard a story about a genie who must transfer jewels from one bottle to another, and who does so by using his staff to pull one of the bottles over to him. In the "magic carpet" group children heard about a genie who solves the same problem by rolling his carpet into a tube and rolling the jewels through it. Children in the control group heard no story.

The children who heard the analogous stories invented solutions analogous to those presented in the stories. For instance, children in the "magic staff" group used the cane to pull the empty bowl closer; those in the "magic carpet" group used the tube to roll the gum from one bowl to the other; in a follow-up study, when not given a tube, children were able to roll up the paper to make a tube.

Several factors constrained performance on this task. Failure by older children was due to not noticing the analogies: when researchers suggested to them that they use the story, the older children had no difficulty solving the problem analogously to the way it was solved in the story. Thus, the eleven-year-olds behaved like the adults in Gick and Holyoak's (1980) study: their problem was not an inability to understand the analogies but rather a failure to notice the analogies. For the younger children (aged four to six), the constraining factor was that the overall mapping had to be complete. That is, the story had to have the same overall structure as the problem situation. When children heard a story with fewer analogical correspondences, they performed poorly. For instance, when children heard a story about a genie whose primary goal was to move into a bigger bottle and share it with a friend, and for whom the transfer of jewels was only an incidental goal, fewer analogical solutions were attempted. This tendency resulted despite the fact that all of the critical elements were still present in the story.

It should also be pointed out that the analogies used here were based partly on physical similarities. We do not know whether preschool children could make use of analogies based entirely on nonsensory similarities (such as reaching out to a lonely person and building a bridge to an island).

Only a few studies have, to my knowledge, investigated the effect of metaphor—rather than analogies—on learning. Arter (1976) showed that passages with metaphor are rated as more important than passages without metaphor, and were better recalled. In contrast, Gaus (1979) and Elam (1979) failed to find an effect of metaphor or simile on recall or understanding of a text. But the evidence that children can benefit from analogy suggests that they also benefit from metaphor provided, of course, that the vehicles of the metaphor come from domains with which they are familiar. Apparently, writers of school texts do not know this, because very few metaphors or analogies are found in school texts (Dixon, Ortony, and Pearson, 1980).

When children begin to produce explicit analogies, the cognitive function of metaphoric thinking is clear: metaphors illuminate the unfamiliar in terms of the familiar. But the metaphors that preschool children invent serve a cognitive function as well. Early metaphoric naming is playful, but it can also be seen as a way of classifying and hence attempting to know and understand the world. The child who called a streak of skywriting a scar was crystallizing her recognition of a similarity between two very different kinds of markings on a surface. The child was clarifying to herself the properties of a novel stimulus, the skywriting, by noting its resemblance to a well-known stimulus, the scar she had so often seen on her mother. This is no less an attempt at organization of the world than is classification on the basis of literal similarity.

• *Restructuring Domain Knowledge*

The role of metaphor and analogy in acquiring information about new domains is well established. A less obvious cognitive function of metaphor has been demonstrated by Kelly and Keil (1984). Consistent with the interaction view of metaphor (Black, 1962), Kelly and Keil present evidence that metaphor restructures our organization of knowledge. Since metaphors link terms from two different domains, it is to be expected that they deepen our perception of the similarity between the topic and vehicle. For instance, after hearing "The *New Yorker* is quiche," our awareness of the similarity between this magazine and this type of food should increase. Kelly and Keil argue further that our awareness of similarity between potential topics and vehicles from the same two domains is also increased. Thus, since the *New Yorker* and quiche are drawn from the domains of periodicals and food, respectively, hearing this metaphor ought to increase the perceived similarity between other periodicals and other foods (the *Wall Street Journal* and spinach; *Seventeen* and cotton candy; *USA Today* and hamburger).

To test this claim, researchers constructed sets of metaphors relating the domains of periodicals and food, and the domains of world leaders and ocean vessels. (An example of the latter was "Nixon is a submarine.") Subjects were first given just the topics and vehicles and were asked to rate each term on Osgood's semantic differential (Osgood, Suci, and Tannenbaum, 1957). Subjects then heard half of the metaphors and were told to rate all the topics and vehicles again. The topics and vehicles from the metaphors *heard* were rated higher in similarity. Thus, the *New Yorker* and quiche were perceived as more similar once the corresponding metaphor had been heard. The topics and vehicles of the metaphors *not heard* also increased in similarity, but only if the resulting metaphors were rated as apt. Thus, the *Wall Street Journal* and spinach were rated more similarly after hearing "The *New Yorker* is quiche." For metaphors rated as poor ("The *New York Times* is cotton candy") the similarity between topic and vehicle decreased. Interestingly, the ratings of the topics changed more than the ratings of the vehicles. This provides support for the claim, discussed in Chapter 2, that it is the vehicle that reshapes our view of the topic, and not the reverse.

Thus, metaphor appears to restructure our organization of semantic domains. Just how long this effect lasts over time, and at how young an age it can be detected, is not known. The effect may apply only when the semantic domains from which the topic and vehicle are drawn are clear. In the examples given above it is clear that the two terms are subsets of the class of periodicals and food. But in a metaphor such as "Your face is an open book," it is more difficult to determine which domains are involved. Body parts and physical objects? If so, the vehicle domain seems too broad for Kelly and Keil's effect to work. Perhaps the two domains are body parts and objects containing symbolically coded information. But here the vehicle domain seems too narrow. Thus, the restructuring effect may occur only in cases with well-defined domains. And whether this same effect can be found in children remains to be determined.

Processing Metaphoric Language

The unique property of figurative language—the requirement that a literal interpretation be avoided—suggests that the comprehension of figurative language may occur in a different way from the comprehension of literal language. One might hypothesize that in understanding any utterance, we begin by trying out a literal reading. If such a reading makes sense, we go on to supplement it where necessary. But if the reading does not make sense, we must reject it and search for a different meaning altogether. A literal reading might be recognized as wrong for one of several reasons: it may be seen to be literally false, as in "Juliet is the sun," or as both false and anomalous, as in "The car died." It may be seen to be both literally true and semantically acceptable but contextually anomalous (as in the example in Chapter 1 in which the wife at the restaurant says, "Things are coming apart at the seams"). Or it may be seen to violate the cooperative principle whereby speakers try to speak in good faith, saying only what they believe to be true and relevant (Grice, 1975).

The claim that metaphor comprehension occurs in stages—that listeners first try out a literal interpretation, recognize that it does not work, reject it, and go on to try a different interpretation—has been used to account for the comprehension of indirect requests (Clark and Lucy, 1975) as well as figurative language (Grice, 1975; Osborn and Ehninger, 1962; Searle, 1979). Grice, for example, suggests that listeners know to reject a literal interpretation only after they first try out such an interpretation and find it defective, because a literal reading would mean that the speaker is violating conversational principles of cooperation.

A testable prediction follows from this model. If figurative language comprehension is a multiple-stage process, then comprehension of metaphors should take more "real time" (reflecting the greater mental work required) than the comprehension of literal language. Studies carried out to test this prediction require subjects to listen to sentences (which are either literal or figurative) and to make some kind of response, as quickly as possible, once the sentence is understood. The measure of interest is whether subjects respond more quickly to literal than to metaphoric sentences.

There is now mounting evidence (using adult subjects) that metaphors do not take longer to process than literal sentences. In one study Ortony, Reynolds, and Arter (1978) presented subjects with brief stories followed by an utterance. In some cases the utterance was intended literally; in others, the utterance was clearly intended metaphorically. For example, the sentence "Regardless of the danger, the troops marched on" followed either a story about military troops (a literal context) or a story about naughty children who persist in misbehaving and ignore warnings of a spanking by their babysitter (a metaphoric context).

The target sentences followed either brief introductions (about six words long) or longer ones of several sentences, totaling about forty-five words. Subjects were simply asked to push a space bar on a keyboard as soon as they had read and understood the target sentence. When the sentences were presented in long contexts, subjects responded as quickly to the metaphors as the literal utterances. Only when the sentences were presented in brief contexts did metaphors take longer to interpret. Thus, subjects did not appear to compute a literal meaning for the sentence, check it against context, reject it, and then proceed to search for a nonliteral meaning. Similar results using this methodology have been found for the comprehension of idioms (Gibbs, 1980; Ortony, Reynolds, and Arter, 1978; Swinney and Cutler, 1979), indirect speech acts (Gibbs, 1979), and irony (Gibbs, 1982, 1986; Rosenblatt et al., 1987). Similar results have also been found for metaphor understanding using a different kind of task: when subjects are asked to paraphrase metaphoric and literal sentences, they initiate the paraphrases as quickly for the metaphors as for the literal utterances (Harris, 1976).

These studies show that we do not first compute a literal interpretation of a metaphoric sentence; if we did, metaphoric sentences would take longer to understand. But it is still possible that during the initial processing of the sentence (before we have arrived at the end of the sentence), a literal meaning of the first metaphorically used word is accessed and then suppressed once the rest of the sentence renders this reading absurd.

There is considerable evidence that when we process a literally ambiguous word ("bank," "cast," "mole"), context guides the selection of an appropriate meaning only after all meanings of the word have been activated (Forster, 1981; Seidenberg et al., 1984; Simpson, 1984; Swinney, 1979). Onifer and Swinney (1981) tested subjects by orally presenting them with sentences containing ambiguous words, as in "For several weeks following the exterminator's visit they did not find a single bug anywhere in the apartment." The term "bug" is ambiguous because it refers to an insect as well as a hidden device for picking up conversations. At the instant that the oral presentation of the ambiguous word ended, subjects saw one of four words flashed on a screen, either "insect" or "spy" (the two meanings of the word "bug") or "custom" or "tan" (control words unrelated to "bug" but matched in frequency to "insect" and "spy"). They were asked to decide whether the letters represented a word (a lexical decision task). Subjects were quicker to decide on "insect" and "spy" than on either of the control terms. Most important, subjects were as quick on "insect" as on "spy," even though the context biased the meaning of "bug" to "spy." Thus, when subjects heard the word "bug," both senses of the word were activated, despite the context.

This effect occurred only when the visually presented word appeared simultaneously with the end of the orally presented ambiguous word. In a second experiment, when the visually presented word was flashed on the screen 1.5 seconds *after* the ambiguous word, only the related word was facilitated in the speed of the lexical decision task. That is, subjects were quicker to decide that "spider" was a word than "spy," when they heard a sentence about using insecticide to kill a bug. Onifer and Swinney conclude that when an ambiguous word is processed in a context which constrains its meaning, *both* meanings are activated, but only momentarily: the irrelevant meaning is lost within 1.5 seconds.

Most studies of lexical ambiguity have shown that when an ambiguous word is processed, context constrains meaning selection only after all meanings have been activated. Onifer and Swinney showed that this constraint occurs within one and a half seconds of activation. If this finding extends to metaphor, we would have to conclude that the temporary activation of both a literal and a metaphoric meaning does not take up more mental processing time than the activation of only one meaning (given the evidence that subjects indicate comprehension of metaphor as quickly as they indicate comprehension of literal sentences). And indeed, if both meanings are activated simultaneously, there is no reason to assume that metaphors take longer to process. It is only if the two meanings are activated sequentially that the argument for more real time is called for.

There is some conflicting evidence, however, suggesting that context may constrain the activation of meanings such that the contextually inappropriate meaning is *never* activated (Glucksberg, 1984; Glucksberg, Kreuz, and Rho, 1986; Simpson, 1981). Glucksberg, Kreuz, and Rho have pointed to a potential problem with Onifer and Swinney's methodology. Instead of "bug" facilitating the visual processing of both "insect" and "spy," perhaps backward priming occurs: that is, the word "spy" facilitates the interpretation of the contextually inappropriate sense of "bug," thus priming a lexical decision for "spy." (See Kiger and Glass, 1983, and Koriat, 1981, for demonstrations of such backward priming.)

To avoid the possibility of backward priming, Gildea and Glucksberg (1983) varied the task so that lexical decisions were made on letter strings which were close to—but not quite—real words. Subjects heard a sentence such as "Even though the outside of the car appeared new, the motor was actually in a very bad state and the mechanic said it would probably need a complete overhaul to work again." Here "state" was the ambiguous word. Lexical decisions were then made on "coundry" (close to "country"), "conbishun" (close to "condition"), or on two unrelated controls. The notion was that "coundry" and "conbishun" would be primed by "state," but not the reverse. And indeed, this was shown to be true, when the decision latencies to the related pseudowords were compared with latencies to the unrelated controls. The correct decision—that the lexical string was not a word—took longer when the pseudoword was related to the contextually appropriate meaning of the ambiguous word, but not when the pseudoword was related to the contextually inappropriate meaning. Thus, hearing the word "state" in a sentence that constrained the meaning to "condition" activated this meaning and hence interfered with the lexical decision that "conbishun" was not a word. And hearing the word "state" in a context indicating the meaning "country" had no effect on a lexical decision about "conbishun." Hence, only the contextually appropriate meanings of the ambiguous words were activated.

If Gildea and Glucksberg's finding holds up, it would suggest either that in processing metaphor with sufficient prior context, the literal meaning may never be activated; or perhaps that the literal meaning is activated only after the metaphoric meaning is activated, in post-sentence reflection. This conclusion would be entirely consistent with the finding that metaphors are processed as quickly as literal sentences.

It is also possible that the findings from literal ambiguity studies cannot be generalized to metaphor, since metaphoric meaning is not always "frozen" in the way the different senses of an ambiguous word are. Thus it seems likely that the literal meaning of a metaphor can never be entirely suppressed. However, whether the literal meaning is activated before, simultaneously, or after the metaphor meaning may well depend on *how* frozen the metaphor is: if the metaphor is highly frozen, the literal meaning should be activated after the figurative meaning; if the metaphor is highly novel, the literal meaning should be activated first; and if the metaphor is intermediate in novelty, the literal meaning should be activated simultaneously with the figurative one.

In an initial study of children's on-line processing of metaphor, Rosenblatt and colleagues (1987) administered a reaction time task to nine- and eleven-year-olds to determine whether metaphors are processed as quickly as literal sentences. Children heard brief stories ending in either a metaphoric or a literal sentence. Each sentence appeared in one context as a metaphor and in another context as a literal sentence, but each subject heard only one context and thus one version of each sentence. The task was simply to press a button as soon as the final sentence was understood. The results were clear. Children of both age groups processed metaphors as rapidly as literal statements. Hence, we can conclude that children process metaphors in the same way as adults: at least for the kinds of fairly simple metaphors used in this study, children immediately (or simultaneously) access the figurative meaning. The context appears to constrain sentence interpretation.

Although it remains unclear at what stage—if at any—a literal meaning for a metaphor is activated, there is evidence that a metaphoric meaning for a metaphor is always activated, and that this activation is automatic rather than optional. Glucksberg, Gildea, and Bookin (1982) have shown that we cannot suppress a metaphoric interpretation of a metaphoric sentence, even when asked only to derive a literal interpretation. Despite instructions to ignore the nonliteral meanings of metaphors, adults automatically derive a metaphoric interpretation while deriving a literal meaning. For instance, asked to decide if sentences are literally true or false, subjects take longer to decide (correctly) that a sentence such as "Some jobs are jails" is false than to decide (correctly) that a sentence such as "Some jobs are snakes" is false. Both sentences are literally false, but the former sentence could also be metaphorically true. Subjects must take longer to decide that this sentence is literally false because the metaphoric interpretation intrudes.

This finding is strong evidence against the claim that we evaluate literal and metaphoric meanings sequentially. We seem to be unable to inhibit a metaphoric interpretation of a metaphoric utterance, at least in the case of semantically anomalous metaphors such as those used by Glucksberg, Gildea, and Bookin. Whether this same effect occurs for whole sentence metaphors (used in a metaphor-inducing context) is not known. It seems probable, however, that the effect would be less likely to occur for such metaphors.

Because subjects do not need to compute a literal interpretation of a metaphoric sentence presented in context, but instead arrive at the figurative meaning by the time the end of the sentence is heard, the comprehension of metaphor should be considered context-driven. In this sense metaphor comprehension is no different from literal comprehension. As Ortony, Reynolds, and Arter (1978) argue, when we hear or read a passage, we automatically invoke schemata which we then use to understand utterances that follow. When we come up against a metaphor in this context, the expectations generated by the context allow us immediately to make sense of the metaphor. For example, if one witnesses an outburst of temper, or reads a description of someone flaring up in anger, one generates abstract schemata such as "destructive," "uncontrollable," and "fearful." A subsequent metaphoric reference to a thunderstorm can then be readily understood in terms of these abstract schemata or associations. The context has generated no schemata about actual thunderstorms, and thus we may never be tempted (or at least never tempted for more than 1.5 seconds) by a literal interpretation; instead we go immediately to an interpretation that fits with the contextually derived schemata.

Clearly, this account only makes sense if there is sufficient context to generate relevant schemata. It is for this reason that metaphors heard in contexts that are extremely spare may well first tempt us to a literal reading of the entire sentence before we achieve an appropriate nonliteral interpretation. Hence, metaphors take longer to process than literal utterances only if they are less related to their contexts. If a literal utterance is insufficiently related to its context, it should take longer to process than a metaphoric utterance clearly related to its context. And indeed, idioms ("let the cat out of the bag") are processed more slowly when they are set in a literal-inducing context (a story about a cat in a grocery bag) than when they are set in a metaphor-inducing context (Ortony, Reynolds, and Arter, 1978). This outcome presumably occurs because the figurative meaning of the idiom is often heard in the context of divulging a secret; in contrast, the literal meaning of the idiom is rarely heard in the context of a cat in a grocery bag.

Thus, we can conclude that in ordinary conversation or reading, metaphors are understood without any special inferential processes unique to metaphoric language. All language comprehension requires going beyond the literal. If we have enough context to go on, we are never led to a literal interpretation of a metaphoric sentence because the prior context constrains our interpretation to the nonliteral meaning. A literal interpretation of a metaphor may be rejected, not avoided entirely. But the literal interpretation seems to be rejected long before the entire sentence has been processed. Hence, metaphors (in context) take no longer to process than literal utterances.

Thus far, I have argued that children possess the competence needed to understand metaphor at least as early as the preschool years. The major constraint on metaphor comprehension in the early years is not metaphoric ability per se, nor is comprehension constrained by the child's level of logical classification skill. Rather, comprehension is limited only by something extrinsic to metaphor—knowledge of the world sufficient to allow mapping of one object onto another very different object, on the basis of similarity.

When errors do occur in metaphor comprehension they most often involve the third step of comprehension, the inference of the unstated meaning. Children are rarely duped into taking metaphors literally, for they do not imagine that the speaker could in any sense mean what he says.

To the extent that metaphor and irony are similar (as two examples of nonliteral language), we should expect children to respond to irony much as they do to metaphor. They should recognize ironic remarks as nonliterally intended even if they infer a meaning not intended by the speaker. And once the task demands are reduced, the ability to understand irony should reveal itself in the early language acquisition years. A very different picture, however, is revealed in the following chapters.

· Chapter 7 ·

How Children Misunderstand Irony

The four-year-old child of a friend of mine announced one day to his mother, "You say 'great' when you're happy and mad." His mother agreed and asked him how he learned that. The child replied, " 'Cause on 'Mr. Rogers' the wolf was selling things and the frog hopped away and the wolf was mad and he said, 'Oh, great.' "

The child's mother brought me this example as counterevidence to the experimental findings which suggest that children cannot understand irony until the age of six or seven. But all that we can conclude from this example is that the child has figured out that a word ordinarily used to indicate a positive feeling can also be used to indicate a negative feeling. On the basis of studies with preschool and early elementary school children, I would venture to guess that if probed a bit, this child would have surprised his mother with his lack of understanding of irony. If she has gone on to ask him *why* the wolf said "great" when he felt mad, the child would probably have simply repeated that you can say "great" either when you're happy or when you're mad, a response perhaps indicating only that he thought the word "great" had two literal meanings. A six-year-old, by contrast, might realize that "great" has only one meaning (a positive one) and that sometimes people say something positive when they feel negative. But if asked *why* the wolf on "Mr. Rogers" said this, the six-year-old is likely to reply that the wolf was trying not to hurt the frog's feelings by showing how he really felt. Such a response would indicate that the child recognized the falsehood in the frog's ironic utterance, and realized that the falsehood was intentional, yet failed to grasp the communicative intention behind the utterance.

The Difficulty with Intentional Falsehood

Investigations of children's understanding of irony usually present children with brief stories ending in ironic statements. The child is then asked a series of questions about the final remark and is considered to have understood it appropriately if he realizes that the remark is false, but avoids taking it as an error or a lie.

In one of the pioneering studies of irony, Ackerman (1981b) investigated children's abilities to detect the intentional falsity of an ironic utterance. He presented children (six and eight years old) and adults with stories ending with statements that were either true, ironic, erroneous, or deceptive. One story was about a character named Billy and Billy's brother, who ran in a race. There was a true version and an ironic version, in which Billy's brother lost the race, and Billy, who had watched the race, said, "I see you won again." This story was also written so that the same final remark was to be interpreted as an error. In this version Billy did not know that his brother had lost the race. Hence, when he said, "I see you won again," he had mistakenly assumed that his brother had won. A sample of the lie version of a story is the case of Robert, who was organizing a baseball game and knew he needed two more players. When his younger brother arrived and asked to play, Robert replied, "Sorry, but we've got too many guys, so you can't play."

The stories were heard on tape, and the final utterances were spoken with the intonation ordinarily used: ironic remarks were made in mocking intonation, and all of the other types in sincere intonation. Subjects were asked three questions about each final statement. For example, for the story about Billy and the race, subjects were asked: (1) Did Billy's brother run well? (a *fact* question); (2) Did Billy know how well his brother had run? (a *belief* question); and (3) Was Billy pleased with his brother's performance? (an *intent* question).

Ackerman analyzed the responses to each question separately. With respect to the fact question, six-year-olds were not as good as eight-year-olds and adults at detecting the inconsistency between the utterance and the facts. Nonetheless, they were able to detect inconsistency at a level above chance for deceptive and ironic utterances. This finding did not hold for erroneous statements: children had particular trouble detecting inconsistency when the inconsistency was *unintentional,* as it was in the error versions. I will return to this finding later; for now, the important point is that even six-year-olds had some ability to recognize ironic utterances as false.

On the belief question six-year-olds responded incorrectly more often than older subjects. This was particularly marked in the case of irony and deception: detection of the speaker's belief was more accurate for errors than for either of the other two kinds of falsehood. That is, it was easier to realize that the mistaken speaker believed what he said than that the ironic or deceptive speaker did not. But a correct answer on the belief question regarding error versions may reflect the default assumption (which usually proves correct) that speakers believe what they say.

On the intent question, both six- and eight-year-olds gave significantly fewer correct answers than did adults for both irony and deception. There was no problem in detecting the speaker's intent in erroneous or literally true utterances, in which cases the correct answer would be to say that Billy was pleased with his brother's performance. Again, it is probably the default solution to assume not only that speakers believe what they say but also that what people say is in line with their feelings and hence is intended literally. Thus, a correct answer on the error items again may not indicate an understanding of errors. Only negative answers to these questions (which would be the correct answers for deception and irony) can indicate for sure that the child understands, because to give a negative answer means to go against the default assumptions of truth, belief, and consistency of utterance with speaker attitude. And indeed, it was on the deception and irony items that children had difficulty with the intent question.

This study documents the difficulty that children have in recognizing falsehood, especially when the falsehood is deliberate, as in deception and irony. Children seem to have trouble accounting for why one would knowingly say something false. One way of resolving such a perceived inconsistency is to render the speaker unaware of the facts. And this is precisely what six-year-olds often did.

Irony versus Deception

In the study just discussed the questions posed do not allow us to distinguish between interpretations of intentional falsehoods as irony or as lies. For both irony and lie interpretations, the replies to the three questions should be the same—that Billy's brother lost (fact), that Billy knew that he lost (belief), and that Billy was not pleased that his brother lost (intent). These are the correct answers whether one thinks that Billy was trying to deceive his brother about his brother's performance (by telling him a comforting lie) or to taunt him (by being ironic). Ackerman's intent question in fact probed the child's understanding of the speaker's beliefs or attitudes, not the speaker's communicative purpose. One can be displeased with something yet not want the person to know. The question did not ask whether Billy was displeased with his brother (and hence inclined to taunt), but rather whether he was displeased with his brother's performance (with the fact that his brother lost).

It is critical to devise questions that distinguish irony from deception, because even when children recognize irony as false and intentionally false, they tend to confuse it with deception (Demorest et al., 1983, 1984). Asked why Billy would say, "You ran a great race" to his brother after he lost the race, children are likely to say that Billy was trying to comfort his brother, to make him feel good, to prevent him from finding out the truth (Demorest et al., 1983).

Demorest and associates noted the tendency to take ironic—but not metaphoric—utterances as white lies. In their study children aged six, eight, and eleven were read stories that ended in one of several types of utterance: sarcasm, metaphor, understatement, hyperbole, irony (defined differently from sarcasm in this study), and a literal remark. The remarks meant to be sarcastic were ones that fit the definition of irony used in this book: positive remarks conveying a negative, critical message. The ironic remarks described an ironic *situation,* that is, a situation in which the opposite of what was expected occurred. On one of the measures used children were simply asked to explain what the utterances meant. Once they had given an answer, they were asked to explain why the person made the remark.

For example, subjects heard a story about a girl named Jane, who was told to clean her messy room. In attempting to clean it, she made an even bigger mess. Here are the final remarks, made by Jane's sister, for each of the five versions of this story:

> Your room looks like it's totally clean now. (sarcasm)
> You have been growing a garden full of weeds. (metaphor)
> Your room still needs a few things straightened up. (understatement)
> Your room is so messy I can't even see you in it. (hyperbole)
> Your room is a mess now after all that cleaning. (irony)
> Your room is very messy. (literal statement)

Children's responses were scored in terms of (*a*) whether they noted that an utterance was false and (*b*) whether they could correctly explain why the speaker said it.

If we consider all of the utterances except literal statements together, we see that children displayed several strategies of comprehension. In 50% of their responses six-year-olds could not even articulate the fact that the utterances were false. Children of this age either gave no response (saying "I don't know"), took the utterance literally (for example, saying "The room was very clean," upon hearing the sarcastic utterance), or ignored the falsehood entirely (saying "She was cleaning in the room," upon hearing the sarcasm). Next in frequency among six-year-olds' responses (29%) were interpretations which made clear that the child knew the utterance was false, but which went no further in trying to explain it. For example, a child might say, "The room was really messy even though she said it was clean." When six-year-olds were able to explain the reason for an utterance, they were as likely to attribute the wrong purpose to the speaker (11%) as the correct one (10%). Wrong purposes were of two types: either the speaker was seen as mistaken ("She's wrong 'cause the room is very messy. Maybe she's blind or something") or the speaker was seen as uttering a white lie ("Jane's sister wanted her to think it was clean so she'd feel better").

Eight-year-olds were more likely to note the falsehood than were six-year-olds. However, although these children noted the falsehood in 46% of their responses, they were rarely able to say anything about the speaker's purpose. When they did note the speaker's purpose, they were again as likely to attribute the wrong purpose (6%) as the right one (8%). Eleven-year-olds were more likely to explain correctly the speaker's purpose than children of any other age group. Twenty-nine percent of their responses included explanations such as the sarcastic speaker was "teasing."

The different types of utterances yielded different frequencies of the various types of interpretation. Children were more likely to note falsehood in the case of metaphor and sarcasm than in the other types of utterance (67% for metaphor and 83% for sarcasm, versus 42% for understatement, 39% for hyperbole, and 28% for irony). Children were also far more likely to explain (whether correctly or incorrectly) the purpose behind sarcasm than metaphor (64% for sarcasm, 13% for metaphor). For example, they were able to say that the speaker made a sarcastic remark "to tease" or "to be mean"; and that the speaker made a metaphoric remark "to say it differently," or "to make a point." When trying to explain the purpose behind sarcasm, six-year-olds said that the speaker was lying or making a mistake in 25% of their responses, whereas eight-year-olds said so in 33% of their responses. Mistake or lie attributions for metaphor were rare: only six-year-olds gave them, and only in 8% of their responses.

This study clearly reveals that the problems children encounter with irony are quite different from those encountered with metaphor. Children fail to realize that the meaning the speaker intends to convey diverges from what he says, assuming instead that the remark is intended to be taken at face value. Because they usually recognize that the utterance is false, they confront a problem, a discrepancy between the recognition of falsehood and the belief that the remark is intended literally. They resolve this discrepancy by distorting either the speaker's beliefs, hence taking the utterance as a mistake, or his intentions, hence taking the utterance as a lie. (In both cases the child has failed at the first step of the scheme presented in Chapter 1.)

In requiring children to explain the meaning and purpose behind the statements, the study posed open-ended questions: What did he mean? Why did he say that? In a subsequent study Demorest and colleagues (1984) developed a more sensitive, less metalinguistic measure of understanding. They framed their questions in such a way that children could give only one of two simple answers, rather than a complex linguistic response.

Children aged six, nine, and thirteen, and adults, were again asked to listen to a set of stories ending with a final remark by one character to the other. Each story was written in four versions: sincere, sarcastic, deceptive, and neutral. One story was about two friends who go to a lake to swim. One dives in and calls out to the other, "C'mon in, the water's warm." In the sarcastic version the water is in fact cold, the diver shrieks, and the final utterance is spoken in an ironic intonation. In the deceptive version the water is cold, but the diver stays calm and speaks in a sincere intonation. In the neutral version the water is cold, but no behavioral or intonational cues are given. Thus, the neutral utterance was ambiguous and could be taken as either deceptive or erroneous. In the sincere version the water is warm.

Children were asked three questions, each with two possible replies. Several open-ended responses were also included, but for now let us consider only the multiple-choice questions. Children were asked a fact question (Was the water warm or cold?), a belief question (Did he think the water was warm or cold?), and a purpose question (Did he want his friend to think the water was warm or cold?). Note that the purpose question was quite different from the intent question posed by Ackerman: Ackerman's question assessed understanding of the speaker's *private attitude,* whereas the purpose question here assessed understanding of how the speaker *intended* his message to be taken *publicly.*

The neutral versions were included to determine subjects' biases. If neutral stories were taken as deceptive more often than ironic, for example, the researchers could conclude that without clues, children assume deceptive rather than ironic motivation, given a false utterance.

By examining the pattern of responses to the three questions, researchers could determine whether an utterance was interpreted as sincere, mistaken, deceptive, or ironic. If a child answered "warm" to all three questions, he showed that he took the utterance to be sincere and true. If he answered "cold" to the fact question but "warm" to the belief and purpose questions, he showed that he took the utterance to be sincere but false—a mistake. If he answered "cold" to the fact and belief questions but "warm" to the purpose question, he showed that he took the utterance to be deceptive. Only if he answered "cold" to all three questions did he show that he took the utterance to be ironic.

Six-year-olds had no trouble interpreting sincere-true remarks correctly. But they had some difficulty with deception (mistaking deceptive utterances for sincere-true ones in almost half of their responses) and with irony (taking these as deceptive in 58% of their responses, and as either sincere-true or mistaken in 36%). Nine- and thirteen-year-olds had no trouble with deception; irony was no longer taken for a sincere remark, but surprisingly it was taken as deceptive in 84% of the nine-year-olds' responses and in 71% of the thirteen-year-olds'. Across ages (including adults), neutral remarks were far more likely to be taken as deceptive (76%) than as ironic (4%), revealing that in children's and adults' theory of mind, deceptive intent is considered more common than ironic intent. Even adults assume a false remark is deceptive unless given explicit intonational or behavioral cues.

These findings demonstrate once again that the problems children have with irony are at step 1. Six-year-olds in this study did not always acknowledge the remarks to be false, and hence took them as literally true. When they did acknowledge the falsehood, they continued to take the remarks literally—as either mistakes or lies. Even nine- and thirteen-year-olds were misled and often mistook irony for deception.

Although in the two studies by Demorest and colleagues children often took irony as deception, there is also some evidence that even six-year-olds can tell the difference between them. In one study children were timed as they decided whether a speaker was making a mistake, telling a lie, or teasing (the term used for irony) (Winner et al., 1986). Children took considerably longer (an average of 0.9 seconds) to decide that an ironic utterance was a lie than to decide that a lie was a lie (0.2 seconds, on average). Thus, children at some level apparently discern the difference between ironic and deceptive utterances, even though they call both such utterances by the same name.

A Problem of Competence or Performance?

The fact that even adults fared so poorly on the task just described suggests that the responses to the questions posed might have underrepresented the subjects' knowledge. The questions posed were difficult and required subjects to reflect about the belief states of the listener. A child who responds correctly to these questions clearly understands irony. But the child who answers incorrectly may do so only because of the difficulty of the task. Just as metaphor comprehension can be demonstrated at a younger age when the task is simplified, evidence for irony comprehension may also be found earlier if the task is made easier. For one thing, in all of the studies discussed above the task places high demands on the subject's memory. To interpret the utterance correctly, the child must *recall* the facts and the speaker's beliefs and behavior as related in the story. Is this task perhaps too far removed from how irony is ordinarily encountered? When irony is encountered in everyday life, children witness a situation that prompts an ironic comment. To understand the comment, they need to be aware of the situation in front of them. They do not need to recall a piece of factual information that was relayed to them in one of a series of stories.

Consider the memory requirements of the swimming story. To respond correctly to the fact question, the child must be able to recall that the water was described in the story as cold. To respond correctly to the belief question, the child must recall the inference that the speaker knew the water was cold. To respond correctly to the purpose question, the child must recall that the speaker shrieked and hence did not try to hide the fact that he was cold.

Suppose that, in the absence of information to the contrary, people naturally assume that utterances are true, sincere, and intended literally. Thus, when an utterance is in fact true, sincere, and literal, subjects can respond correctly simply by falling back on default assumptions. Identifying a remark as ironic requires that the child recall three pieces of information: the facts, the speaker's knowledge, and the speaker's behavioral and intonational cues signaling whether or not he wants his utterance to be believed. To identify a remark as deceptive, the child must recall only two pieces of information: the facts and the speaker's knowledge. And to identify a remark as an error, the child must recall only one piece of information: the facts. If the child forgets information about the speaker's belief or intention it does not matter, again assuming that the default assumption to be that the speaker believes what he says and intends his remark literally.

These requirements constitute the memory component of irony comprehension tasks as ordinarily presented. On this analysis understanding irony in a story in which information is presented sequentially requires more memory than does understanding deception; deception requires more than errors; and errors more than literally true utterances. Studies which use the paradigm described above and which conclude that irony is more difficult to identify than deception may have confounded comprehension with recall. Only by reducing the memory demands in the comprehension task can we determine whether failure to understand irony is due to memory limitations or to more conceptual limitations.

A second difficulty with the task as ordinarily presented may be the questions asked to assess comprehension. In particular, the question used to assess understanding of the speaker's intention toward the listener is difficult because it is embedded, that is, one must reflect about what the speaker wanted the listener to think. A simpler measure might dispense with the three questions altogether in favor of simply asking children to label the utterances as lies, mistakes, or teasing.

Along with four colleagues, I recently carried out a study in which we examined the contribution of memory demands and difficult questions to the child's misunderstanding (Winner et al., 1987). We devised a low memory demand condition and compared children's performance on this task to their performance on the task as usually administered. We also compared comprehension as assessed by labeling (as lying, making a mistake, or teasing) with that assessed by probing the child's understanding of the facts, the speaker's beliefs, and the speaker's purpose.

We assigned five-year-olds to either a situation or a story condition. Subjects in the situation condition were given a low memory demand task. They witnessed live interactions between two adults that ended in an ironic, deceptive, or mistaken utterance. Subjects in the story condition were given the standard, high memory demand task. They heard stories describing the same interactions, and the stories ended with one of the characters uttering an ironic, deceptive, or mistaken remark. In both conditions, utterances were spoken with the intonation that typically accompanies such utterances: errors and lies were spoken in ordinary, sincere intonation; irony was spoken in mocking intonation.

Here is what a child would typically experience in the situation condition, for example. He is brought into a room and is seated at a table with two adults. Adult 1 tells the child that together they are going to play a guessing game with Adult 2.

The child is seated next to Adult 1, and across the table from Adult 2. The guessing game will be played three times. Four flashcards are held up for all three participants to see. On one side of each card is a picture: either a blue square, a yellow triangle, an orange circle, or a red star. Adult 1 then turns the cards face down and announces that she will pick one of the cards, and Adult 2 will have to guess which card she has picked. Adult 1 proceeds to pick the blue square and shows it to the child but not to the other adult. "Guess what's on my card," she challenges the other adult.

In the irony version, Adult 2 makes a wrong guess—the orange circle. Adult 1 holds up the blue square for all three participants to see, and smirks and says, in mocking intonation, "Yeah, it's the orange circle." In the deception version, Adult 2 guesses correctly. Adult 1 then shows the card to the child, but keeps it hidden from the guesser and tells a lie: "Nope, it's the orange circle," she says sincerely.

In the error version, Adult 2 guesses incorrectly, saying, "The orange circle." Adult 1 then shows Adult 2 and the child that she is in fact holding the blue square. In all three versions the child is privy to the same information as Adult 1: whatever this adult sees, the child does.

Notice the difference in the task for children in the story condition. Here is the story corresponding to the above interactions: "Tom and Meg liked to play a game with cards. The cards had different pictures on them. Each picture was a different color. There was one with a blue square, one with a yellow triangle, one with an orange circle, and one with a red star. Meg had to guess which card Tom was holding. On one turn, Tom had the card with the blue square in his hand. He hid the card from Meg. 'Guess what's on my card,' Tom said." In the irony version the story continued as follows: " 'The orange circle,' said Meg. Tom showed Meg his card. Tom said, 'Yeah, it's the orange circle.' " In the deception version the story continued: " 'The blue square,' said Meg. Tom kept his card hidden. Tom said, 'Nope, it's the orange circle.' " And in the error version: " 'The orange circle,' said Meg. Tom showed Meg his card. Tom said, 'Nope, it's the blue square.' "

After each episode children were asked the same three questions posed by Demorest and associates (1984). For example, regarding the irony item described above, children were asked a fact question ("Did Tom have the blue square or the orange circle?"); a belief question ("Tom said he had the orange circle. Did he really think he had the orange circle or did he think he had the blue square?"); and a purpose (or literalness) question ("Tom said he had the orange circle. Did he want Meg to think he had the orange circle or not?"). As in Demorest and colleagues' 1984 study, we collated responses to these three questions to determine whether an utterance was interpreted as literally true, mistaken, deceptive, or ironic.

Children in the situation condition had to depend much less on their memory than those in the story condition. Those in the situation condition did not have to remember which card the speaker was actually holding (to determine whether the utterance was true or false); they did not have to remember whether the speaker could see which card it was (to determine whether the falsehood was intentional or accidental); and they did not have to remember whether the person with the card had hidden the card or had shown the card to the guesser (to determine whether the falsehood was intended as irony or deception). There was no need to hold these facts in memory because the events were enacted in front of the child. At the same time that the target utterance was spoken, the child could see which card was being held and whether the speaker could see the card.

We felt that the situation condition mirrored as closely as possible the natural contexts in which children encounter irony—in social interactions, rather than through dialogue in stories. To mirror natural life even more exactly, a researcher ought to address ironic remarks *to* children in a given situation. Since this cannot be done (for ethical reasons), we chose the next best alternative: addressing ironic remarks to another person in the child's presence.

After being questioned on the three items used in this task, the items were presented once again. This time children were asked whether the speaker was lying, making a mistake, or teasing (a labeling measure). By comparing how children performed on the two measures, questions and labels, and by comparing performance in the story and situation conditions, we were able to determine the role of the response mode and of memory demands in understanding irony.

This study showed that memory demands cannot explain children's difficulty in understanding irony. We found no significant difference in the frequency with which irony was understood in the two conditions. (In fact, subjects actually achieved higher mean scores in the situation condition!) Deception was understood equally often by both groups. Errors, however, were understood much better in the situation (58%) than in the story condition (29%), and this difference did prove significant. It appears that detection of verbal error places high demands on the subject's memory, perhaps because children must remember that an utterance is false when there is no apparent motivation for the falsehood. Thus, performance on error tasks can be improved if memory demands are reduced. But neither detection of irony nor deception was facilitated by reducing the memory requirements. This suggests that failure to understand irony is not simply an artifact of the way the studies have been carried out. Instead, misunderstanding irony appears to reflect a genuine conceptual confusion about why someone would knowingly say something false yet not intend to deceive his listener.

The response mode used made a difference, but only when the items were heard in story dialogue rather than witnessed directly. Children performed equally well (averaged across the three utterance types) in the situation condition with either measure. But in the story condition, children performed significantly worse on the three questions than on the labeling measure. It is thus possible that the use of the three questions combined with the story format underrepresents children's knowledge.

It is important to emphasize that even in the easiest task (situation condition; labeling measure), five-year-olds responded to irony at chance level (25% on a three-choice measure). Chance level performance was found even among six-year-olds in another attempt to facilitate comprehension (Winner et al., 1986). In that study children were asked to pretend they were in the situation that resulted in the ironic comment. For instance: "Pretend your friend Michael decided to make some peanut butter cookies. Pretend some of the cookies got burned. You came in and took a bite of one of the yucky burnt cookies and said, 'You make yummy peanut butter cookies.' " Final utterances were spoken in mocking intonation, and children were then asked, "When you said that, were you making a mistake, kidding around and teasing, or telling a lie?" When questioned about what was meant by the label "kidding around and teasing," most of the children said this meant "being mean." In responding, children scored no higher than chance level—1.5 out of 3.0. Thus, children did not see the critical attitude underlying the ironic remarks: not only did they not recognize them as nonliteral, but they also did not recognize them as critical.

It appears that preschool children fail to integrate the conflicting components of an ironic utterance. Irony presents the child with a blatant contradiction: the speaker is saying something that he neither believes nor means. Faced with this contradiction, young children either distort the belief to fit the statement (resulting in an interpretation of irony as error) or fail to acknowledge that the speaker means to convey something different from what he says (resulting in an interpretation of irony as deception).

The consistent finding that preschool children cannot demonstrate irony comprehension contrasts strikingly with research revealing metaphor comprehension by children as young as three, four, or five, under optimal conditions (Gardner, 1974; Gentner, 1977; McCarthy, Winner, and Gardner, 1980; Vosniadou and Ortony, 1986). I return to a discussion of possible reasons for the greater difficulty of irony in the concluding chapter, in which metaphor and irony comprehension are directly compared.

The Role of Intonational and Behavioral Cues

Irony is typically accompanied by a special intonation. The intonation may be sarcastic (mocking, exaggerated, contemptuous); it may be flat (deadpan); or it may be overly sincere. The intonation is usually inconsistent with the content of the utterance. That is, if the statement is positive, the intonation is either downright negative, subtly negative by its flatness, or so overly positive as to alert suspicion. Metaphor is uttered in no special kind of intonation; neither are erroneous or deceptive statements. An error is said in the same way as sincere-correct utterances, since this is the kind of utterance that the speaker thinks he is making. And the speaker who lies attempts (though he may fail) to keep his intonation consistent with his utterance: he does not signal his true beliefs with an intonation that conflicts with what he says. Hence, intonation may serve as a cue in detecting and making sense of irony, but is less useful for other kinds of false utterances.

Irony is also typically accompanied by certain kinds of behavioral cues: the speaker is likely to indicate his negative attitude either by a negative facial expression (smirking, rolling his eyes) and/or by negative bodily gestures (pointing, making a fist). Because metaphor does not function to convey a negative attitude, it is not typically signaled by any special kinds of facial expressions or gestures. Errors, of course, are not accompanied by such cues, since the speaker does not know he is uttering a falsehood, and deception is also free of such blatant cues, since the speaker does not want his deception to be discovered (see Ekman, 1985, for a discussion of the inadvertent cues to deception).

The role of intonational and behavioral cues in understanding irony has been investigated in several studies. Let us first look at the effect of such cues on adults. Winner and Gallagher (1983) asked adults to listen to tape-recorded stories ending in either irony or deception. In the behavior-voice condition, stories contained behavioral information (such as "he pointed," "he laughed"), and the utterances were presented in mocking, sarcastic intonation. In the behavior condition, only behavioral information was given: both irony and deception were spoken in neutral, flat intonation so that intonational cues could not be used to distinguish them. In the intonation condition, intonational but not behavioral cues were supplied. Subjects were asked the fact, belief, and purpose questions posed by Demorest and her colleagues (1984).

It was expected that irony but not deception would be facilitated by the presence of cues; that the presence of both types of cues together would facilitate comprehension the most; and that intonational cues would facilitate understanding more than behavioral cues, since the intonational cues were heard directly, whereas the behavioral cues were described verbally and thus experienced only indirectly. Moreover, intonational cues were predicted to be less ambiguous indices of irony than were behavioral ones: a speaker might laugh or point yet not be ironic; but if a sarcastic intonation is used, the utterance must be ironic.

The findings were clear. Although understanding of deception was unaffected by condition, this was not true for irony. Irony was understood most often in the behavior-voice condition, as one might expect since this condition contained two types of cues whereas the other conditions contained only one. Most interesting is the comparison between the behavior and the voice conditions. Contrary to expectation, behavioral cues proved more informative than intonational cues, despite the indirect method by which behavioral cues were presented. The finding that behavioral cues are perceived as more indicative of ironic intent than vocal cues may mean that behavioral cues are more salient. But I find this implausible. It seems more likely that listeners detect both types of cues equally well but have difficulty *interpreting* intonational cues.

One reason understanding irony may require more cues than deception is that there seems to be a bias toward assuming that the speaker wants the listener to believe what he says. This bias was noted in the frequency with which irony was mistaken for deception, by the adults in both this study and the 1984 study by Demorest and associates. The presence of more than one cue suggesting that the speaker does not want the listener to believe what he says seems to be necessary to counteract this bias.

• *Does Intonation Help Children?*

To investigate whether children can make use of intonational cues, Winner and colleagues (1987) compared comprehension of written and spoken utterances. Children aged six, eight, and ten viewed videotapes of interactions ending in irony, hyperbole, and understatement. The final utterances were either spoken in appropriate intonation (the intonation condition) or they were presented in print on the screen and had to be read by the subjects (the written condition). Because of reading limitations, the written condition was presented only to eight- and ten-year-olds. Irony was spoken in a negative, mocking intonation. Hyperbole was spoken in an exaggerated intonation consistent with the meaning of the utterance. Since the meaning was always negative, the intonation was extranegative. And understatement was uttered in a slightly flat intonation, which was considered consistent with the meaning of the utterance, since an understatement downplays an event.

It was assumed that intonation would facilitate comprehension, and that intonation would be more helpful for irony than for hyperbole or understatement. The latter prediction was made for the following reason. The intonation cue in irony conflicts with the meaning of the words: the words convey a positive meaning, the intonation a negative one. This conflict does not occur in hyperbole, where the words convey exaggeration as does the intonation. Nor does it occur in understatement, where the words and intonation downplay the speaker's meaning. Attention to the intonation in irony should alert the child to the fact that the speaker means something different from what he says, and hence is not uttering a lie.

Once again, comprehension was measured through responses to questions about facts, beliefs, and intentions. When performance in the oral and written versions was compared, no difference was found. Surprisingly, children understood irony as well when it was presented without intonation as when it was accompanied by a mocking tone. In addition, intonation had no effect on the understanding of hyperbole and understatement. This finding is consistent with the observation that adults are helped less by intonational than behavioral cues (Winner and Gallagher, 1983). Still, it is surprising that intonation did not help at all. Perhaps it is not the ineffectiveness of intonation but the *measure* of effectiveness that accounts for this finding, since the eight-year-olds in this study almost always understood the ironic utterances, and thus the true effect of intonation could not be measured. (The children in the study may have shown irony comprehension at an earlier age because the episodes were presented visually rather than read aloud. Whether intonation facilitates comprehension in younger children could not be determined by this study, since six-year-olds did not receive items without intonation.) Although understatement and hyperbole were less well understood by children aged eight, one must bear in mind that intonation is a less informative cue for such utterances since it is not inconsistent with the literal content of the statement. Hence it is not surprising that intonation did not help in understanding hyperbole and understatement.

These results are somewhat consistent with those reported by Ackerman (1983a), who compared comprehension of ironic utterances spoken in stressed, negative, and neutral intonations. Although Ackerman found that the stressed intonation did facilitate comprehension to some degree in both six- and nine-year-olds, he also reported that context was a much more powerful cue than intonation. That is, when the context clearly suggested an ironic interpretation, children were helped more than when the intonation suggested such an interpretation. Ackerman also noted that eight-year-olds found stressed intonation more helpful than six-year-olds did.

The finding that six-year-olds make less use of intonational cues than do older children suggests either that they do not fully discriminate the intonation, or that they do not know how to interpret it. It seems much more reasonable to conclude the

latter—that children simply do not know that a mocking intonation signifies that the speaker does not mean what he says.

• *The Cues Children Rely On*

In the 1984 study by Demorest and colleagues, described above,
children were asked "How do you know?" after they had answered each of the three (two-choice) questions. Thus, researchers obtained information about the kinds of evidence
children used—or thought they had used—to determine the
facts, the speaker's beliefs, and the speaker's purpose. The key
issue was whether children would justify their decisions by referring to the literal content of the utterances (hence using
noninformative cues), by referring to the facts of the situation
(which would fail to distinguish between deception and irony),
or by referring to cues that would differentiate irony and deception (the behavioral information contained in the stories and/or
intonation in which the utterances were spoken).

There were two major findings of interest. First, both children
and adults mentioned more reliable cues when justifying their
judgments of speaker belief than when justifying assessments of
speaker purpose. To determine speaker belief (and hence to
distinguish between sincere and intentionally false utterances),
the facts are the most informative cue, and this was the most
common cue mentioned by subjects of all ages (cited by roughly
50%). To determine speaker purpose (and hence to distinguish
between irony and deception), the most reliable cues are the
speaker's behavior and tone of voice. Instead of relying on these
cues, both children and adults were most likely to fall back on
the statement itself as evidence. The fact that subjects used more
reliable cues to judge belief than purpose is consistent with the
finding that children are more able to distinguish sincerity from
deliberate falsehood (and thus to judge belief accurately) than
to distinguish among deliberately false remarks (and thus to
infer purpose accurately).

Second, reliance on more informative cues in judging belief

increased with age. Appeals to the statement declined with age, whereas appeals to behavioral and intonational cues increased with age. Similarly, in gauging a speaker's purpose, subjects increasingly (with age) used behavioral and intonational cues.

The responses were then broken down by type of utterance, so that the types of cues subjects appealed to in discerning deception and irony could be compared. To distinguish deceptive from sincere remarks, one must appreciate that the speaker's belief is inconsistent with his statement. Those who recognized deception judged speaker belief correctly by relying on the facts of the story and not the statement. But those who misinterpreted deception misjudged the speaker's belief by relying on the statement, thus taking the remark as sincere.

To distinguish deceptive from ironic remarks, one must identify the speaker's purpose. The speaker's belief is the same for both utterance types. Thus, it is not surprising that subjects who misinterpreted irony judged belief by cues as valid as those used by subjects who interpreted irony correctly. It was in judging the speaker's purpose that accurate and inaccurate interpreters of irony relied on different cues. Those who understood irony relied most often on behavioral cues; those who misunderstood irony appealed to the uninformative cue of the literal content of the statement.

It is interesting that subjects who misunderstood irony were able to use behavioral cues correctly to determine that the speaker's belief was inconsistent with the statement, but were unable to use these very same cues to recognize that the speaker's purpose deviated from his statement. Subjects noticed that the speaker's behavior was discrepant from the content of his statement, and they used this behavioral cue to judge speaker belief. But they did not rely on behavior to judge speaker purpose. Thus, when a speaker's behavior is inconsistent with his statement (as it is in irony), children are apt to see this behavior as evidence of the speaker's belief, but not as an intentionally manipulated cue to signal disbelief to the listener. Children seem to assume instead that the speaker's statement reflects his purpose, and that his behavior is unintentional. Children, it would appear, feel that a speaker can control his words more than his behavior.

Children rarely said that they relied on intonation to determine speaker purpose. Once again, intonation proved to be less informative than behavioral cues. Taken together, these studies point to the counterintuitive conclusion that sarcastic intonation is less useful in distinguishing irony from deception than the speaker's gestures and/or facial expressions.

Processing Irony

As discussed in Chapter 6, even children can process metaphors directly (without first testing a literal meaning), if the metaphors are understandable and given sufficient context. Using a reaction-time paradigm, experimenters have demonstrated that adults process ironic utterances directly also (Gibbs, 1986).

Rosenblatt and colleagues (1987) investigated this issue with children by comparing ironic utterances spoken in mocking, sarcastic intonation with those spoken in deadpan intonation. The subjects were nine- and eleven-year-olds, and adults. Subjects heard brief stories ending with either ironic or literal utterances. The stories were written so that each final statement could be understood as either ironic or literal, depending on the context of the accompanying story. For example, the sentence "We're having a terrible thunderstorm" concluded, in the literal version, a story about two people who cancel a barbeque because of a forecast (which turns out to be accurate) of foul weather; in the ironic version of the story the forecast is incorrect, and the weather turns out to be beautiful. In this way each final statement was matched for structure and complexity across literal and ironic utterances.

Subjects heard ironic utterances spoken in one or the other intonation and were told to press a button as soon as they felt they understood the final utterance. Later, comprehension was tested by asking the children to paraphrase the final utterance.

Reaction times for all items that were paraphrased incorrectly were excluded from the analysis.

The results were surprising. Among adults, ironic utterances in mocking intonation were actually understood *more* quickly than literal utterances. And ironic utterances in deadpan intonation were processed as rapidly as literal utterances. These findings clearly demonstrate that, as with metaphoric statements, the context of an ironic utterance can lead the hearer directly to the speaker's intended meaning; the literal meaning need not be accessed first. Although not statistically significant, there was a tendency for children to process ironic utterances in mocking intonation more quickly than either deadpan irony or literal utterances. When irony is spoken in mocking intonation, the intonation may be so potent a cue that the hearer grasps the speaker's meaning faster than in the case of literal utterances.

This last observation may appear to conflict with the finding, reported earlier in this chapter, that intonation does not facilitate comprehension in children. But the two results can be easily reconciled. While intonation may not play an important role in comprehension, it may indeed play a role in the speed of processing an utterance that the child is already able to understand.

Social Functions of Irony

Understanding speaker meaning in an ironic utterance is not enough. Full understanding also requires some sense of the effect of irony on the hearer, as well as the motivation of the speaker in choosing irony over a literal form of discourse. In several studies researchers have asked subjects to compare ironic and literal remarks to determine what people perceive to be the differences between using irony and a literal *equivalent*. Particular attention was paid to the possibility that irony is chosen over a literal equivalent because it is more biting, more funny, and more status elevating. These possibilities were examined with various forms and intonations of irony.

Of the set of studies conducted by Kaplan and associates (1987), the first involved adults only and tested the perceived aggressiveness of irony. Subjects were read stories ending in one of four remarks: an ironic insult, in which the speaker says something positive to mean something negative ("You're going to look great in your picture," said to someone wearing garish clothes for his school photograph); a literal insult ("You're going to look awful in your picture"); an ironic compliment, in which the speaker says something negative about a positive situation ("You really have no dancing talent at all," said to someone who just gave a successful performance); and a literal compliment ("You sure know how to dance"). Subjects were then asked to rate the aggressiveness of each remark on a five-point scale, ranging from −2 (very very insulting) to +2 (very very complimentary).

Contrary to the authors' hypothesis, literal insults were rated as more aggressive than either form of irony. Irony, then, is not chosen over a literal equivalent because it is more biting; rather, it seems to be chosen because it is a milder form of criticism. By speaking indirectly, the speaker mutes his attack. Ratings for ironic compliments were as negative as those for ironic insults, showing that even when a speaker says something negative to mean something positive, he never just means something positive but always means something critical as well. Thus it appears that irony twists the effects of literal discourse: an attack becomes *less negative* if phrased in the form of irony; and praise becomes *less positive* if phrased in the form of irony.

In a similarly designed study, adult subjects were asked to rate the speaker's status relative to the addressee (the victim of the irony) and to rate the humor of the utterance. In each case subjects were asked to compare an ironic insult with its literal equivalent, and an ironic compliment with its literal equivalent. Although the speaker using the ironic insult was perceived to be superior to his addressee, so also was the speaker using a literal insult. In fact, no difference was found between the perceived status of the speaker of an ironic insult and that of the speaker of a literal insult. In the case of ironic compliments, the speaker was perceived to be the equal of the addressee—not his superior. And of course the speaker of a literal compliment was perceived to be inferior to the addressee. These results show that speakers do not choose an ironic insult over a literal equivalent in order to elevate their status with respect to the addressee: either form of utterance will do that. They do choose an ironic compliment over a literal one if they want to elevate their status. An ironic compliment, however, is less status elevating than an ironic insult.

With respect to humor, both forms of irony were perceived as funnier than literal forms of speech. And ironic insults were rated as funnier than ironic compliments. These results allow the following conclusions. Adults perceive irony to be a way of muting rather than intensifying a critical comment; irony is a way of saying something in a funny way; but irony is not more likely than a literal insult to increase the speaker's status.

In a study that included children, Kaplan and her associates examined the perceived humor and aggression in several forms of irony spoken in several kinds of intonations. Children aged six and eight, as well as adults, participated in this study. Subjects heard stories ending with three possible final remarks: a literal insult and two forms of ironic insult, direct and indirect. Direct irony statements expressed the opposite of the speaker meaning; indirect irony statements by one inferential step expressed the opposite of the speaker meaning. The ironic utterances were presented in either a "boast" or a "no-boast" context. In the boast contexts ending in direct irony the victim of the irony made a boast ("I always bake great cookies"), which was then shown to be unjustified (he burned the cookies); another character then mimicked the boast ("You always bake great cookies"). In the boast context ending in indirect irony the speaker did not echo the boast but said, for example, "These cookies will be perfect for the party." In the no-boast stories the direct irony was in the form "You sure are a graceful diver," said to someone who had just done a belly flop; and the indirect irony was again one inferential step away ("I guess diving's going to be your favorite class"). Ironic remarks were spoken in one of three intonations: mocking (the kind used in almost all studies of irony), deadpan (flat, neutral), and mock-sincere (exaggeratedly positive). Subjects were asked to decide which of the three endings for each story was the meanest (or most aggressive), and which was the funniest.

First, the aggression ratings. Consistent with the results of the earlier study, irony was perceived to be less mean than literal insults, and this was true for both adults and children. Intonation contributed to the perceived aggression in irony: mocking intonation was perceived as the most mean, followed by deadpan intonation. Mock sincere intonation was perceived as the least mean. Whether the irony was direct or indirect had no effect on perceived meanness; and whether or not the irony mentioned a previous boast also had no effect on judgments of nastiness.

As for the humor ratings, irony of all types was perceived as funnier than literal insults, again confirming earlier results. Although subjects of all ages rated irony as funnier than literal insults, humor ratings for irony increased with age: adults almost never found literal insults the funniest of the three remarks; children sometimes did. In terms of intonation's effect on humor, the mock sincere intonation was considered the funniest, perhaps because such utterances have two properties that are incongruent with the speaker's beliefs and the facts—the utterance and the intonation. Hence there are two incongruities: that between intonation and the facts, and that between utterance content and the facts. The indirectness of the irony also affected perceptions of humor. Among the six-year-olds, direct and indirect irony were equally funny; among eight-year-olds, indirect forms were slightly funnier; among adults, indirect forms were always funnier. Finally, whether the irony mentioned a previous boast affected humor ratings. For six-year-olds, the utterances which mimicked the boasts were funnier than the more indirect forms, which did not; for eight-year-olds there was no difference; and for adults, the irony which did not mimic the boast was the funniest.

We can conclude that children are sensitive to some of the social effects of irony—they perceive irony as a milder form of criticism than a direct insult, and they respond to the humor of irony. But children tend to perceive the most obvious forms of irony as funniest (direct irony, and irony that echoes a previous boast), whereas adults perceive subtler forms as funnier.

Irony presents several problems for children. At the most elementary level, children have difficulty detecting the falsehood of irony. Even more difficult to detect is the intentionality of the falsehood. Most problematic is the task of detecting whether the speaker intends the falsehood as deception or as irony. Unlike metaphor, irony is misunderstood by children at step 1, when they take it as false but literally intended, in other words, as a mistake or lie. It is even possible that for irony, step 3 can be solved before or without recognizing the speaker's nonliteral intent. (I am indebted to Giyoo Haetano of Tokyo University for this suggestion.) Support for this hypothesis comes from a recent pilot study in which children (aged six and seven) were asked to discriminate between literal and nonliteral utterances as well as to interpret the nonliteral utterances (Kaplan, Winner, and Rosenblatt, 1987). Depending on their condition, children either had to distinguish between metaphoric and literal speech, or between ironic and literal speech (a step 1 task). They also had to interpret the nonliteral utterances (a step 3 task). In the case of metaphor, children were able to perform the discrimination task better than the interpretation task, showing that they succeeded at step 1 but not 3. Just the reverse was true for irony: children were somewhat better at interpreting the speaker meaning than in hearing irony as a special way of speaking, different from literal usage. This suggests that one can catch the speaker's intended message in irony without even realizing that the speaker has conveyed his message indirectly. But full understanding of irony (as well as metaphor) requires that the listener not only understand the speaker meaning but also be aware of the utterance as an indirect, nonliteral form of speech (Olson, 1986).

· Chapter 8 ·

Constraints on Irony Comprehension

Given the kinds of comprehension errors children make, it would appear that the constraints on irony comprehension are very different from those on metaphor comprehension. The skills that constrain irony comprehension are the abilities to discriminate falsehood from truth, to infer another's beliefs, and to infer another's intentions. The ability to note falsehood is necessary in order to avoid taking irony as literally true. The ability to infer beliefs is needed if one is to avoid taking irony as a mistake. And the ability to detect intentions is needed to avoid confusing ironic with deceptive intent. But whether any of these skills are *sufficient* for the avoidance of these errors is an empirical question.

Detecting Incongruities

To avoid taking irony as literally intended, the listener must detect some kind of incongruity between what is said and the facts of the matter. As long as the incongruity is between an utterance and facts that are publicly observable, the detection of incongruity requires no inference at all. All that is required is vigilance. When I say, "It's nice that the sun is out," as our picnic is destroyed by a rainstorm, my drenched companions know that the sun is *not* out. Detecting this kind of incongruity requires monitoring rather than inferential skills. In contrast, detecting incongruity between stated beliefs and private beliefs requires inferential ability. For instance, when I say "I love rain on a picnic," the incongruity is only noted if the hearer is able to *infer* my true beliefs. Similarly, when Hamlet says "Thrift, thrift," the reader must infer that he does not believe this to be the motivation for the marriage. Hence, it should be easier to detect incongruity when the utterance contradicts a public rather than a private state of affairs.

Children can detect *nonverbal incongruity* at a very young age. An early form of this ability is seen in the one-year-old's delight at the game of peek-a-boo: the surprising incongruity between appearance and disappearance is clearly detected and found to be funny. Thus, children have the capacity to detect nonlinguistic incongruity long before their comprehension of irony is in question.

By age four, children can detect the *incongruity between an utterance and a public fact*: at this age children can reliably judge whether an utterance is true or false. Wimmer, Gruber, and Perner (1984), for example, presented children with a story about a girl walking along a path perpendicular to a high garden wall. As she approached the wall, she saw a lion in front of it. A younger girl was in the garden behind the wall and could see only the animal's tail. The younger girl behind the wall asked what animal it was. The older girl, who could see the lion, told the other girl that it was a dog (a lie). Children were asked whether this was true. Almost all four-year-olds realized not only that the reply was false but also that it was a "fib." The story then continued. The younger girl was asked by her brother what animal was behind the wall. When the girl told him it was a dog (an unintentionally false statement), four-year-olds also recognized that this was false. The fact that four-year-olds have the ability to detect falsehood when an utterance contradicts a known fact suggests that children of this age should be able to detect the falsehood of irony when the ironic utterance contradicts a public, knowable fact.

The ability to detect the *logical incongruity between factual statements* emerges considerably later than the ability to detect the incongruity between a proposition and a situation. Markman (1977) investigated sensitivity to logical inconsistencies in spoken instructions. In one study children aged six, seven, and eight were asked to evaluate instructions that contained glaring omissions. Unless actually asked to carry out the instructions, or shown partial demonstrations of the instructions, six-year-olds failed to detect the omissions. In a second study Markman (1979) read brief passages containing either explicit or implicit logical contradictions to children aged eight, ten, and eleven. In a story with an explicit contradiction it was reported that fish living at the bottom of the ocean cannot see because there is no light. The very next sentence stated that the fish know what to eat because they can see the color of their food. In a story with an implicit contradiction the text simply stated that there was no light at the bottom of the ocean, and then reported that fish living there know what to eat by identifying the color of their food. Children were then probed extensively for their understanding of the story and whether it made sense. Markman found no differences in the responses from children of different ages: all children, including the oldest, had considerable difficulty with this task, even with the explicitly stated incongruities.

Thus, children are sensitive to nonverbal incongruity in infancy; when as young as four years of age, they can detect the incongruity between an utterance and a fact; but the ability to detect logical incongruity between two statements made by one voice—that of an impersonal narrator—seems not to develop until well into the school years.

- *Incongruity in Irony*

On the basis of these findings, we can predict that the ability to detect the falsehood of an ironic utterance which is incongruous with the facts should emerge in children no younger than four. This much is obvious. The question of interest, however, is whether the ability to detect falsehood in irony should emerge as soon as children have shown the ability to detect incongruity between an utterance and a fact, or whether there is a lag between the emergence of the ability to detect falsehood in a mistake or lie and the ability to detect the falsehood in irony. It is possible that irony poses a specially difficult case of incongruity detection for children. If children detect that an ironic utterance is false, but cannot understand *why* someone would say something so blatantly false, they may distort the facts to fit the utterance. In this case children would deny the falsehood in an ironic remark because they cannot make sense of it.

The evidence suggests that there is indeed such a lag. Conti and Camras (1984) investigated the ability of children aged four, six, and eight to detect ironic violations of Grice's (1975) maxim of quality (that we say what we believe to be true). For instance, in a story in which the weather is said to be cold, one character says, "It sure would be a nice day to go to the beach." Other maxims were also violated, yielding remarks that could be taken as ironic but which were not false. The maxim of quantity, for example, was violated by a character who replies to the question "What do you want to be when you grow up?" with insufficient information: "I want to be an adult." The maxim of relevance was violated in a story in which a man needs help fixing his car. His neighbor offers to help, but when asked what he will do to help, the neighbor replies, "I will go take a nap." And the expectation that a request will be reasonable (see Gordon and Lakoff, 1971) was violated in a story in which a boy goes to visit his friend who has a broken arm and asks the friend to "come out and play baseball."

Children were asked to select the "funny or silly" ending. Four-year-olds performed at chance level: only three out of the sixteen four-year-olds selected ten out of twelve violations as funny, the level necessary to exceed chance. In contrast, 83% of the six-year-olds and 100% of the eight-year-olds performed above chance level. The type of principle violated did not affect incongruity detection: children able to recognize a violation of the maxim of quality (the type most often violated in irony) could also recognize violations of the other types, and children unable to recognize a violation of quality could not recognize violations of any other type.

Four-year-olds may have performed at chance not because

they failed to detect falsehood but because they did not find the falsehood either funny or silly. In another study using a different methodology, however, children this age and younger were again shown to be unable to detect ironic incongruity (Ackerman, 1981a). In this study kindergartners, first graders, and second graders heard brief stories ending with a character's reply to a question. In three quarters of the items the reply violated a conversational rule: either the rule of contingency (that speakers discuss the same topic of conversation), the rule of relevance, or the rule that conversations should be informative. In the remaining quarter the reply conformed to all of these rules. An item violating the rule of contingency described a scene in which a boy responded, "I wonder what time it is?" to a friend's request to borrow money. An item violating the rule of relevance showed a girl replying, "The popcorn was alright" when asked about a movie she had just seen. An item that was not informative described a girl who, looking at her brother's newly painted purple bicycle, asked, "Did you really paint the bike purple?"

The task was to decide in each case whether the reply was made by a truthful character (Honest Alice) or by a character who was a "smart aleck" and liked to fool people (Saucy Sally). Whereas 84% of the first and second graders were able to discriminate between the utterances that violated and those that conformed to the maxims, only 39% of the kindergartners were able to do so. Although the youngest children performed better on this task than on Conti and Camras's (perhaps because of the factor mentioned in the previous paragraph), their ability to detect this kind of incongruity was shown to be poor.

Another line of evidence that children fail to detect the incongruity in irony long after they have developed the ability to detect verbal incongruity comes from the interpretation errors reported in the previous chapter: misinterpretations of irony as literally true, though not as prevalent as other forms of misinterpretation, persist through the age of six (Ackerman, 1981b; Demorest et al., 1983, 1984). But children seem to have more trouble detecting incongruity in deception than in irony (Demorest et al., 1984), perhaps because of the cues to incongruity that accompany irony but not deception (negative intonation and facial expressions). And children seem to have more trouble detecting the incongruity in an unintentionally false utterance than in either deception or irony (Ackerman, 1981b; Winner et al., 1987). This last finding may reflect the fact that an unintentionally false utterance is not deliberately false, whereas irony and deception are. Possibly an awareness of the speaker's motivation underscores the falsehood; when no intention to be false is noted, children may assume that in fact no falsehood has been uttered. I return to the different problems posed by deliberate and accidental falsehood later in this chapter.

• *Why Literal Interpretation Errors Persist*

There are at least two other possible explanations for the persistence of literal interpretation errors, in addition to the explanation I have already suggested (that children may detect the falsehood but fail to understand the motivation). Memory failure and the kinds of cues children use to decide whether a speaker is credible or not may also be factors.

The role of *memory* in the detection of incongruity was investigated by Ackerman (1982), who manipulated the position of the critical utterances to be judged, placing them either before or after the stated story facts. In addition, the facts and the ironic utterances were positioned either adjacent to each other or separated by one sentence. For example, one story was about a boy named Billy who was making a lot of noise at school. The ironic utterance was spoken by his teacher: "You're very quiet today, Billy." This utterance was placed either before or after the statement about Billy's noisiness; and it was either adjacent to this statement or separated by one sentence.

The children tested were six and eight years old. Unfortunately for our purposes, children were not asked directly whether the utterances were true or false. Instead, they were asked an intention question: regarding the story just described, for instance, they were asked whether the teacher wanted Billy to stop talking. If children replied "Yes" to this question, we can infer that they recognized the falsehood of the irony. But if children replied "No," we cannot infer that they failed to recognize the falsehood, since they may have interpreted the utterance as a lie: perhaps the teacher wanted Billy to feel that he was behaving well.

The critical manipulation appeared to be the separation between the fact statement and the ironic utterance, rather than the order in which these two statements appeared. If the ironic utterance was separated from the context by one sentence, six-year-olds performed at chance level, whether or not the context followed the utterance. Eight-year-olds performed at chance level when the nonadjacent ironic utterance came after the facts (the order almost all studies have used), but improved when the statement of facts followed the irony. If the utterance and facts were adjacent, performance was not affected by the order of the sentences. When the utterance was said after a statement of the facts (so that children had to hold the facts statement in memory), performance declined. These results are entirely consistent with those reported by Winner and colleagues (1987) and discussed in the previous chapter: five-year-olds detected errors much more easily when the false utterance was spoken *while* the child could observe the facts.

Thus, interpretations of irony as literally true may be an artifact of the way the studies are typically carried out. In studies of irony comprehension children are presented with texts describing both the facts of a situation and a character's response. As Markman (1977, 1979) found, detecting logical incongruity in verbal texts is difficult for children: as they concentrate on what they hear, they seem to forget what came before. Ackerman's study suggests that this also happens when children are asked to detect incongruity between an utterance and a statement of the facts in a verbal text.

In "real life" children first encounter irony in face-to-face interactions rather than in verbal texts. The fact that memory problems are part of the problem in incongruity detection as normally investigated suggests that children may detect the incongruity in an ironic utterance said *to* them even when they fail to detect it in an ironic utterance said by one character to another in a verbal text.

The role of *credibility cues* in the detection of incongruity was also investigated by Ackerman (1983b), who found certain cues that children attend to more than others in deciding whether or not an utterance is false. Attention to the wrong kinds of cues can lead children to ignore the falsehood in an ironic remark.

In this study six- and eight-year-old children heard stories in which a direct utterance (in quotation marks) made by either a child or an adult contradicted an indirect statement (not in quotation marks) made by either an authoritative or a nonauthoritative source. Here is one of the stories children heard: "Jack was in the third grade but he hadn't been in school for three days. The hospital announced that Jack's family had a new baby boy. Ralph walked in his house. He wanted to buy a present for the baby. His little sister who knew Jack's family said, 'Did you know that Jack has a new baby sister?' "

In other conditions instead of the hospital making the indirect statement, the announcement was made by "the janitors" (a nonauthoritative source). And the speaker was either a child (the little sister, as above), or an adult (Jack's mother). The speaker was always someone familiar with the person talked about; the indirect source was not. In all stories the authoritative source was supposed to be more credible than even the adult speaker, and the nonauthoritative source was meant to be less credible than even the child speaker. The key issue was whether children's tendency to believe a statement is affected by the speaker's authority, age, or familiarity with the person he is talking about.

Adults were influenced most by the authority of the source: they believed the source over the speaker when the source was authoritative; they believed the speaker when the source was nonauthoritative. Whereas eight-year-olds followed this pattern to a lesser extent, six-year-olds remained uninfluenced by the authority of the source. Instead, six-year-olds were most affected by the age of the speaker, believing the adults more than the children. Thus, Jack's mother was more believable than his little sister, and the mother was equally believable whether she contradicted the janitors or the hospital source. Although children are sometimes willing to contradict an adult (Flavell et al., 1981; Patterson, Massad, and Cosgrove, 1978), this study shows that young children assume a person to be more believable simply because of age. But age is of course a less informative cue than the authority of the source. In contrast to the six-year-olds, eight-year-olds used both age of speaker and authority of indirect source as credibility cues. And adults were influenced only by the authority of the indirect source.

Six-year-olds were also more likely overall than older subjects to believe the speaker over the source. This tendency did not occur because the speaker's utterance came last, as evidenced by a subsequent manipulation in which Ackerman reversed the positions of the quoted and the indirect utterances. Although there was some effect of recency, six-year-olds remained more likely to believe the speaker—no matter what—than did adults. Ackerman argues that children believed the quoted utterance because they tend to believe what a friend would say over the testimony of a stranger. But whether children are also biased to believe a direct over an indirect quote was not tested: direct quotes by story characters were always pitted against indirect quotes by some anonymous institution (the hospital) or individual (the janitors).

Although the stories used in this study did not make clear whether the falsehoods were intentional or unintentional, the findings may supply some clues about children's detection of falsehood in irony. Children seem to be influenced by uninformative cues: the age of the speaker; the familiarity of the speaker with the person discussed; to some extent the recency of the information; and possibly the way the utterance is presented—as a direct or indirect quote. This suggests that children should be prone to believe and take literally a false utterance spoken by a person who knows the person he is making reference to, if the speaker is an adult, if the utterance is the last thing heard, and if the utterance is made directly by a story character rather than reported by a narrator. Thus, difficulty with incongruity detection arises not because children lack the ability to detect incongruity when it is pointed out to them, but rather because of the information-processing demands of tasks that make use of verbal texts, and because of a tendency to use uninformative cues as indicative of credibility.

Detecting Beliefs

Inferring the speaker's beliefs is important in understanding irony for two reasons. First, in cases where the ironic utterance asserts or implies a subjective opinion, such an inference is critical in order to determine whether the utterance is true or false. Second, even when the ironic utterance is objectively false, it is necessary to infer the speaker's belief to determine whether the utterance is intentionally or unintentionally false. Thus, whether children can recognize the distinction between intentional and unintentional acts, and whether they can infer a speaker's belief in order to determine whether a false utterance is intentionally or accidentally false, are abilities we must examine.

• *Intentional versus Unintentional Actions*

The belief that an understanding of intentionality is late to develop was put forth by Piaget (1932) in his studies of moral development. Piaget investigated children's understanding of intentionality by studying their moral judgments of actions that varied in two ways: in how negative a consequence resulted (for example, breaking fifteen cups versus breaking one); and in whether or not the consequence was a result of an ill-intentioned act (breaking the fifteen cups in an innocent accident as opposed to breaking one while trying to sneak jam out of the cupboard). Piaget asked subjects to decide which of two described children had been "naughtier." He found that children under seven years of age judged naughtiness on the basis of consequence rather than intention. Thus, breaking fifteen cups was a naughtier action than breaking one, even if the one was broken as a result of a naughty act and the fifteen were broken entirely by accident.

This study has been interpreted as demonstrating that children under seven years of age lack the concept of intentionality. But all that we can conclude from this study is that the concept of intentionality is not relevant for children's moral judgments. And even this conclusion is suspect. The actions in Piaget's stories always entailed some form of property damage. Subsequent studies have shown that while children do use consequence more than intention as a basis of moral judgment, the use of intention increases if the stories involve personal injury rather than property damage (Berg-Cross, 1975; Berndt and Berndt, 1975; Elkind and Dabek, 1977; Karniol, 1978).

Children understand intentionality long before they consistently make use of it in moral judgments. Children as young as age three can distinguish between intentional behaviors and unintentional behaviors, such as reflexes, passive movements, and mistakes (Shultz, Wells, and Sarda, 1980). Moreover, five-year-olds can make fine distinctions about what is intended—distinguishing between intending an act and intending a consequence of that act (Shultz and Shamash, 1981). And in both these studies children were as successful at judging others' intentions as they were their own.

Children as young as age five are able to use two informative cues in deciding whether an act is intentional: how positive the outcome of an act is, and how much the actor monitored his behavior (Smith, 1978). If the outcome is positive for the actor, and if the actor has monitored himself, then the behavior is more likely to be deemed intentional.

• *Intentional versus Unintentional Verbal Falsehoods*

Although even very young children possess the conceptual distinction between intentional and unintentional behavior, they may fail to distinguish between intentional and unintentional verbal falsehood. What is critical here is the ability to infer the speaker's beliefs about the facts. If the speaker's beliefs accord with the facts, then a false remark should be seen as intentionally false; but if a speaker's beliefs do not correspond to the facts but rather correspond to what he says, then a false remark should be seen as unintentionally false. As early as age two, children spontaneously talk about people's desires and beliefs (Bretherton and Beegly, 1982). They use epistemic verbs such as "to know," and they understand whether a person knows or does not know something. To distinguish intentional from unintentional falsehood, however, children must be able to do more than this. They must be able to reflect about beliefs and recognize them as subjective states different from objective truth (Olson and Astington, 1985). In addition, children must be able to attribute *false* beliefs to others, and must know when to attribute a false belief and when to attribute a true belief to another person.

Since we typically share access to the same facts, we typically share beliefs, and the unmarked condition is to assume mutual (and true) knowledge: that what I know is known by others, and that others assume that what they know is known by me (Schiffer, 1972). Given this situation, to understand someone's behavior we do not usually need to infer anything about his beliefs, since by default we assume the person's beliefs to be the same as ours and hence true. It is only in the marked condition—when an incongruity between an utterance and the facts has been detected—that we need to decide whether the person's beliefs are true or false.

Studies have examined children's abilities to take the perspective of another person and recognize what that person does or does not know. These studies have demonstrated that children as young as two and a half can represent the difference between their own and another person's epistemic relation to the same object (Flavell, 1978; Flavell, Shipstead, and Croft, 1978; Lempers, Flavell, and Flavell, 1977). Children of this age understand that another person can see an object behind a screen, even though the object is not visible to the child. By age four or five, children can understand something about the difference between their own and another person's epistemic relation to the same propositional content (Chandler and Greenspan, 1972; Flavell et al., 1968; Marvin, Greenberg, and Mossler, 1976; Mossler, Marvin, and Greenberg, 1976). These studies have shown that children can understand that they know something that another person (usually a story character) may not.

Somewhat more difficult for children is the understanding that they know one thing and a story character (falsely) thinks the opposite. That is, the ability to represent another's false belief emerges after the ability to represent another's ignorance (Hogrefe, Wimmer, and Perner, 1986). But it is the ability to detect a false belief that is critical in identifying error and hence avoiding taking irony as unintentional falsehood. This ability was investigated by Wimmer and Perner (1983). In their study children were told a story about a child named Maxi, who puts some chocolate into a blue cupboard. In his absence, his mother moves the chocolate to a green cupboard. Children were asked where Maxi will look for the chocolate. They can only answer this correctly if they are able to determine Maxi's belief, which is wrong and different from what the subject knows to be true.

Four- and five-year-olds pointed incorrectly to the actual location of the chocolate—they pointed to where they knew the chocolate really was. Only children aged six and older were able to point to the wrong location, demonstrating that they were cognizant of Maxi's wrong belief. Thus, by six years of age, children can attribute a wrong belief to a story character. It follows that by this age they ought to be able to recognize unintentional error and to distinguish it from intentional falsehood.

As discussed in the previous chapter, however, even eight-year-olds who recognize the falsehood of an ironic remark sometimes fail to realize that the remark is *intentionally* false (Ackerman, 1981b; Demorest et al., 1983, 1984). Thus, they take the ironic remark as an unintentional error. Recall the children who thought that the statement "Your room looks like it's totally clean now," when said by the sister looking at Jane's messy room, perhaps meant that the sister was blind (Demorest et al., 1983). Such interpretations occur when subjects wrongly attribute a false belief to a speaker. We know from Wimmer and Perner's research that by age six children should be able to attribute a wrong belief to someone when it is appropriate to do so (as in the Maxi story). What we see with irony is that children possess this ability but apply it incorrectly. That is, they attribute a false belief to the speaker when in fact the speaker possesses a true belief. This may well be the child's solution to the conflicting components of the situation. To resolve the contradiction, children sometimes alter the facts to fit the statement, and thus take an ironic utterance as true. Another solution to the perceived contradiction is to alter the speaker's belief to fit the false statement, and thus to take the ironic statement as erroneous.

According to Wimmer and Perner's conclusions, children find it easier to attribute a true belief than a false belief to someone. Moreover, since the subject in the experiment knows the truth, it should create less dissonance to attribute the same knowledge to the speaker than to attribute a belief to the speaker that contradicts that held by the subject. All of this suggests that children should recognize the speaker's beliefs more frequently when the speaker has uttered an intentional falsehood such as an ironic statement (since the speaker's beliefs are then "true" and also in line with the subject's) than when the speaker has uttered an unintentional falsehood (since the speaker's beliefs are then false and contrary to the subject's).

Oddly, just the opposite occurs. Children have more difficulty determining a speaker's belief when the utterance is intentionally rather than unintentionally false. Ackerman (1981b) found that both six- and eight-year-olds answered a question about the speaker's beliefs at chance level for deception and irony, but not for unintentionally false utterances. Thus, while they correctly recognized mistakes as unintentionally false, they incorrectly classified irony and deception also as unintentionally false. It seems that there is a period when, whatever the utterance, children are vulnerable to the error of assuming that the speaker of a false remark is unaware of the falsehood. Children have no difficulty recognizing the discrepancy between their own beliefs and those of a speaker. Their difficulty lies in recognizing the discrepancy between a speaker's statement and beliefs—that is, in realizing that one can assert something one does not believe. Faced with such a puzzle, children alter one variable of the equation, the speaker's beliefs, so that the speaker is perceived to be saying what he believes. The difficulty seems to be that children do not fully understand the communicative purpose behind intentional falsehood.

Detecting the Speaker's Communicative Purpose

Even if an utterance is recognized as contrary to the speaker's beliefs, and thus as intentionally false, the listener still faces the challenge of determining the speaker's communicative purpose. The listener must decide whether the speaker intends to hide his true beliefs and hence to convey the literal meaning of his utterance (in which case the speaker is trying to lie), or whether the speaker intends to reveal his true beliefs and hence to convey the nonliteral meaning of his utterance.

As with the task of detecting the speaker's beliefs, detecting the speaker's purpose requires inference. To determine speaker purpose, one can sometimes rely on the *mode* of the utterance— its intonation, its accompanying facial expressions and gestures. If the speaker is being ironic, he may adopt a deadpan or mocking tone, and he may sneer or smirk. But such clues may not be available: irony may be encountered in written form, or an ironic speaker may "pretend" to sound and look sincere (as in the mock-sincere intonation discussed in the previous chapter). One must then rely on other clues—whether the speaker has often lied in the past (whether he is a deceptive person); whether there is a motive for the speaker to lie about what he is saying; whether the speaker and addressee have a relationship sufficiently intimate to permit kidding; and, perhaps most important, whether the speaker knows what the listener knows about the matter. If the speaker who says, "Great day for the beach," knows that the listener also heard the prediction for rain, then we can rule out deception. One does not lie when there is no chance of being believed. But if the speaker believes that the listener does not know the facts (he has not yet heard the prediction), then we cannot rule out deception on this basis alone but must rely on some of the other cues just mentioned.

There are two skills critical for the detection of motivation and hence for distinguishing irony from deception: understanding different kinds of motivational states, including the motivation to deceive; and inferring second-order beliefs, the speaker's beliefs about the listener's state of knowledge.

• *Understanding Motivational States*

Even very young children understand something about internal motivational states. Three-year-olds, for instance, are able to predict how people will behave if their motivational states are explicitly described. In one study children of this age were able to predict which of two children would play with a set of blocks more—the one described as "interested" in the blocks (or "wanting to play" with the blocks) or the one less interested in (or less desirous of) playing (Miller, 1985). These children were as adept at predicting the effects of internal states on behavior—degree of interest, intelligence, motivation, effort—as they were at predicting the effects of external states, such as parental pressure and visual distraction. This study provides evidence that at least by age three, children possess the concept that internal motivational states direct actions. If children are told about the internal state of a character, they are able to engage in causal reasoning with respect to this internal state.

Whether such young children are able to infer motivational states spontaneously is a different issue. There is some evidence that this skill develops after age six. When children were given filmed social episodes and asked to describe them, they focused on the physical appearance and behavior of people, not on their implied internal characteristics (Flapan, 1968). When asked to match passages from the *Iliad* that could be grouped either on the basis of external similarity (characters wearing similar clothing) or on the basis of implied internal states (anger, fear), children under age seven matched on external cues (Damon, 1967). And, when given fairy tales from which descriptions of motivational states had been deleted, six-year-olds in a delayed recall task repeated the story just as they had heard it, whereas eleven-year-olds added the implied motivations (Rubin and Gardner, 1985). Thus, while the *ability* to think about internal states is present in very young children, and while children as young as two years of age use epistemic verbs such as "want," preschool children *prefer* to focus on external rather than internal characteristics of people.

Most important for our purposes is the question of when children can understand the two different motivations behind lying and being ironic. We know little directly about either children's or adults' understanding of the motivation to be ironic (though studies discussed in the previous chapter shed light on children's and adults' understanding of the effects of irony). But we do know something about children's understanding of the motivation to deceive. And presumably, once children understand why someone lies (and the situations in which one does so), they should realize that an ironic utterance is something different from a lie.

In Wimmer and Perner's Maxi study, children were asked not only where Maxi would search for the chocolate, but also where Maxi would tell his brother to look. Subjects were told that Maxi's brother wanted the chocolate, but that Maxi did not want him to get it. Once children were able to understand that Maxi was mistaken about the location of the chocolate, they were also able to predict Maxi's deceptive behavior— Maxi should point to the correct location in his effort to deceive his brother. This understanding emerged in children six years old. Thus, by age six children can not only predict deceptive behavior (given an explicit statement of a deceptive goal by the experimenter), but also can predict such behavior on the basis of a false belief. Surprisingly, it was no easier for children to construct a lie on the basis of a correct belief than on the basis of a false belief.

It is not until between the ages of five and six that children can spontaneously infer a deceptive plan, given an utterance by a story character. Wimmer, Gruber, and Perner (1984) presented children with fairy tales containing two main characters. The goals of these characters were described, and the two goals were clearly in conflict. This was followed by a critical utterance on the part of one of the characters, an utterance implying a deceptive plan. Only 28% of the four- and five-year-olds were able to judge the critical utterance as a lie; but by age five and a half, children generally realized that the utterance was a lie.

Simply because children were able to say that the critical utterance was a lie does not allow us to conclude that they understood deceptive motivation. Piaget (1932) found that six- and seven-year-olds called mistakes with no deceptive intentions "lies." Wimmer, Gruber, and Perner (1984) confirmed this "lexical realism" on the part of young children. When children heard mistakenly false utterances, they recognized them as well intentioned (they felt the speaker should be rewarded for being nice rather than punished for being nasty) but still called the utterances lies. Even when children were able to infer a mistaken speaker's belief (and hence realized that the speaker was unaware of the facts), they still said the speaker was lying. Thus, despite the fact that even four-year-olds use intention in moral judgments, they do not use intention in their definition of what it means to lie. Even some eight- and ten-year-olds made this error.

Perhaps a better indicator of children's understanding of deception, one which does not rely on a verbal understanding of the term "lie," comes from nonverbal studies of their understanding of deceptive behavior and of their own deceptive behavior toward others. If children themselves demonstrate deceptive behavior, they may well be able to infer such behavior in another person. Children's deceptive behavior has been investigated in games in which it is to the players' advantage to try to deceive each other. For example, Shultz and Cloghesy (1981) devised a card-hiding game, the object of which was to determine whether the experimenter was holding a red or a black card. The experimenter either pointed honestly to red (indicating that he had the red card) or switched to a deceptive strategy (pointing to black when he had the red card). The assumption was that if children detected the deception on the part of the experimenter, they would adopt the strategy of guessing the opposite color from the one pointed to by the experimenter. Five-year-olds modified their guessing, indicating they realized that the experimenter was being deceptive. Three-year-olds, however, did not. When children were placed in the pointing role, they were much less likely to behave deceptively than they were to detect deception on the part of the experimenter. Nonetheless, there was some evidence of deceptive behavior initiated by children as young as five.

A study by Ackerman (1985) confirmed Wimmer, Gruber, and Perner's finding that children can infer deceptive intent by age six. Moreover, Ackerman identified one of the conditions facilitating such inference. Children aged six and eight heard stories containing a final utterance. In half of the stories the context strongly suggested that the utterance was a lie; in the other half, the context was ambiguous so that the utterance seemed false but might have been true. For instance, one of the stories strongly suggesting a lie was about a child named Billy who had watched television until 10:00 P.M. and had forgotten to do his homework. The next morning he announced, "I don't think I should go to school today because I feel a little sick." The corresponding ambiguous story simply stated that Billy had watched the television show and made the announcement the next morning. His forgetting to do his homework was not stated. Children were asked an open-ended question ("Why did Billy say that?") and were also asked explicitly whether Billy was lying. Regarding both of these questions, there were significantly more deception responses from eight-year-olds than from six-year-olds. Nonetheless, when the context clearly implied that the story character was lying, six-year-olds recognized the final utterance to be deceptive in 78% of their responses.

Since children as young as five or six detect the difference between the intention to lie and the intention to tell the truth, and since children by age five attempt to deceive others, their misinterpretations of irony as lies cannot be due to a misunderstanding of the motive to deceive. Instead, perhaps, children fall back on such interpretations because they do not have any other way of explaining why someone would say something that is deliberately false. Another possibility is that children fail to detect the speaker's beliefs about the hearer's beliefs, and hence genuinely believe irony is deception.

• *Identifying Second-Order Beliefs*

To attribute to someone a belief about the objective world is to attribute a first-order belief. To attribute to someone a belief about another person's belief state is to attribute a second-order belief (Perner and Wimmer, 1985). Any form of intentional falsehood requires second-order beliefs, both for its production and for its detection.

To understand that a remark by one person to another is intended deceptively, a third party must entertain a hypothesis about the speaker's beliefs about the hearer's beliefs. That is, the liar is someone who knows the truth (a first-order attribution) and who thinks that the hearer does not know the truth (a second-order attribution) and hence will not see through the lie. The liar says, "The weather is great," only to someone who does not know that it is in fact raining; and the liar says, "I think dyed hair looks great," only to someone who does not know that the speaker hates dyed hair. Moreover, the liar must make a second-order gamble: he must gamble that his utterance will have an effect on the hearer's beliefs, that the hearer will believe the false utterance.

To understand that a story remark is intended ironically, the child must entertain a different hypothesis about the speaker's beliefs about the hearer's beliefs. The ironist is someone who knows the truth and who thinks that either (*a*) the hearer also knows the truth and will thus recognize the speaker's true intent as critical or (*b*) the hearer will recognize the speaker's true meaning and will thus recognize the speaker's critical intent. The speaker intending to be ironic says, "The weather is great," only to someone who knows that it is raining, or to someone who the speaker thinks will see through the utterance and realize that the weather is not great. And he intends his praise of dyed hair ironically only if he knows that the hearer knows (or will realize from the utterance) that the speaker dislikes dyed hair.

A series of studies by Perner and Wimmer (1985) demonstrates that until somewhere between the ages of five and eight, children make errors in attributing second-order beliefs to story characters. In these studies children were presented with a story in which two characters initially share knowledge about the location of an object and then both see the object moved. Although both characters know where the object has been transferred, the first character thinks that the second character has a false belief about the location of the object. The task was to determine where the first character thinks that the second character will go in search of the object. The subject knew where the object *really* was but had to ignore this in his response and think only about where the first character wrongly thinks the second character will go.

For example, in one story, John and Mary are in a park and together they see an ice cream van. Mary goes home to get money for the ice cream. John stays at the park and sees the van leave. The ice cream man says he is going to park in front of the church. Hence, John knows where the van is going, but he assumes that Mary does not know. However, Mary has seen the van driving by her house. She asks the man where he is going and he tells her he is going to park at the church. Since John does not know that Mary talked to the man, he continues to think that Mary falsely believes the van is in the park. He goes to Mary's house and is told that she went for ice cream. So he goes to look for her. Subjects are asked where John will go to look for Mary.

The correct answer is the park. This can only be determined by entertaining a second-order belief: John thinks that Mary thinks the van is in the park. A reply that he went to the church demonstrates first-order belief attribution: either that Mary knows the van is at the church (and thus went to the church) or that John knows the van is at the church (and thus went to the church). This reply may also demonstrate zero-order belief attribution in that it may simply reflect what the subject knows (the van is at the church).

Most seven-year-olds and half of the eight- and nine-year-olds gave first-order strategy responses, replying that John went to the church. Most of those aged ten could give second-order strategy responses. The age of acquisition of second-order beliefs was slightly lower when memory demands were reduced. For example, when the critical question was posed immediately after the statement that John did not know that Mary had talked to the ice cream man, 25% more of the responses were correct. Perner and Wimmer conclude that children develop the competence to entertain second-order beliefs between the ages of five and eight, but that in the absence of facilitation, children may revert to first-order beliefs until between eight and ten years old.

These findings would seem to have strong implications for children's understanding of irony. Children who interpret irony as error are making the first-order belief attribution that the speaker has a false belief. They need consider nothing about the speaker's beliefs about the hearer's beliefs. Children who correctly detect errors as errors also need only make first-order belief attributions. Children who interpret irony as deception are making second-order belief attributions, but they are attributing the *wrong* second-order belief to the speaker. Thus, children may take irony as error when they fail to make second-order attributions; and they may take irony as deception when they attempt a second-order attribution but get it wrong. Perhaps children get it wrong (and hence take irony as deception) in part because they are practicing the new skill of second-order belief attribution.

In brief, there are three underlying abilities necessary to interpret irony correctly. To avoid taking irony as literally true, the child must detect incongruity or falsehood; to avoid taking irony as error, the child must correctly attribute beliefs to another mind; and to avoid taking irony as deception, the child must infer motivation and be able to attribute second-order beliefs accurately. The concept of belief, so problematic for children, seems to be necessary for comprehending irony but not metaphor, which is one of the reasons, as is discussed in the concluding chapter, why metaphor comprehension develops first.

Chapter 9

Why Children Understand Metaphor before Irony

I have argued that children interpret the two chief forms of nonliteral language in qualitatively different ways. Despite the parallels between each in terms of the steps required for comprehension, step 1 (detecting the utterance as one in which sentence and speaker meaning diverge) is the major stumbling block in irony comprehension, whereas step 3 (detecting the speaker meaning) is the problem in metaphor comprehension. Hence, the most common misinterpretation of irony is to take it as literally intended but false (as a mistake or a lie); the most common misinterpretation of metaphor is to take it (correctly) as an indirect way of conveying a message but then to infer the wrong message.

A study in which children's comprehension of metaphor and irony were directly compared on the same task provides further support for the claim that these forms of nonliteral language call on qualitatively different abilities (Andrews et al., 1986). Six- and eight-year-olds were asked to make sense of utterances that in one context were interpretable as metaphors ("There sure isn't any pepper in the soup," said about two children too tired to play) and in another context were interpretable as irony (the same statement made by a customer at a restaurant when served soup heavily seasoned with pepper after he had specifically requested no pepper). Children were asked about the speaker's intent (was he making a mistake, telling a lie, teasing, or saying something in a different way?). They were also given multiple-choice questions about the speaker's meaning (for example, for the metaphoric example given above, the correct choice was "The children weren't excited"; for the ironic usage, "There was pepper in the soup").

As predicted, irony was often taken as a literal falsehood (a step 1 error), whereas metaphors were recognized as a means of "saying something in a different way," probably because the metaphors were highly implausible as errors or lies. But with the metaphors there was a disjunction—that did not occur with the ironic statements—between understanding the speaker's intent and understanding his meaning. Even when six-year-olds realized the speaker was talking in a different way, they often remained confused about what he meant. Thus, they succeeded at step 1 but failed at steps 2 and 3, as in the study by Kaplan, Winner, and Rosenblatt (1987), described in Chapter 7. In the case of irony, once children realized the speaker was teasing, they understood his meaning. That is, once they made it past step 1, they solved steps 2 and 3. Therefore, for children, detecting that there is a divergence between what is said and what is meant is more difficult in irony than in metaphor. Once children recognize this, however, they comprehend the meaning of irony more easily than the meaning of metaphor. Moreover, as shown in the study by Kaplan and associates, it is even possible to grasp the meaning of irony *without* recognizing a divergence between what is said and what is meant.

Given the striking difference in the errors that these two non-literal forms yield, and given the different cognitive skills underlying the comprehension of each form, there is little reason to conceive of nonliteral comprehension as a unitary skill. The ability to understand metaphor is independent of the ability to understand irony, and there is reason to expect that understanding irony is the more difficult of the two skills. As is argued below, I believe that irony is more difficult because only irony requires its listener to have an awareness of the concept of belief.

Studies discussed in Chapters 3 and 4 demonstrate metaphor comprehension in children at least as young as four years of age if the comprehension task is made as easy as possible, and if the child has some understanding of the topic and vehicle of the metaphor. Studies discussed in Chapter 5 show that children as young as three or four are also able to produce metaphors (albeit primitive, rudimentary ones). And studies reviewed in Chapter 6 suggest that metaphor, if understood, serves the same cognitive function for children as for adults—to explain, clarify, and illuminate. A very different picture emerges of irony comprehension, one suggesting that until children acquire a full understanding of the status of beliefs, at about age six (according to Olson and Astington, 1985), they cannot understand irony, even if the task demands are reduced.

Let me first discuss what I mean by an awareness of beliefs. The philosopher Donald Davidson (1984) argues that consciousness of one's beliefs as beliefs has three features: (1) One must have a concept of a belief as a belief, as something distinct from external reality; (2) One must realize that because a belief is distinct from external reality, it could be false; (3) One must have awareness of other mental states, because to believe is only one of many propositional attitudes one can entertain (others, for example, are doubting, intending, and forgetting).

We know that by age three children use mental verbs such as "know," "think," and "pretend" (Bretherton and Beeghly, 1982; Shatz, Wellman, and Silber, 1983), and that children are capable of realizing that thinking about an object is different from actually possessing it (Wellman and Estes, 1984). There is no evidence however, that children this young realize that a belief may be false and, hence, that two people can hold different beliefs about the same thing, or that an individual could hold different beliefs about the same thing at different times. It is precisely this type of awareness that would seem to be critical for irony comprehension.

Olson and Astington's (1985) study suggests that this ability is in fact lacking in children until sometime between the ages of six and nine. Olson and Astington tested children aged five, six, and nine, using a set of paper cut-out animals: two were the same color—a blue dog and a blue pig; two were of different colors—a red cat and a green horse; and one, a yellow cow, was not shown. The animals were placed behind a paper barn with two windows that opened and closed. When the windows were opened, two color patches were revealed, but the shapes of the animals were not visible. Children were asked two questions: "What do you see?" and "Do you know what animal it is?" In response to the first question, children were supposed to give a color name; to the second question the correct answer was "yes" if the color was red or green, "no" if it was blue (since there were two animals that color), and "no" if it was yellow (since children had never seen the yellow animal).

Children revealed a strong tendency to confuse their perceptions with their beliefs, and their beliefs with the truth. Half of the responses to the first question, from children of all ages, gave an animal name, thus revealing a confusion of percept with belief. In response to the second question, all five-year-olds said "yes" to the blue patch, whereas only 40% of the nine-year-olds said they knew what the blue patch was. Regarding the yellow patch, 31% of the five-year-olds said "yes," whereas only 13% of the nine-year-olds responded this way. Thus, older children distinguished more clearly than younger children between the unambiguous pair (red cat, green horse), for which it was correct to say "yes," and the ambiguous pair (blue dog and pig), for which it was correct to say "no."

Researchers then introduced a doll, who was said to have never seen the animals outside the barn, and asked the same questions about the doll's sight and knowledge. In this case it was always correct to answer "no" to the second question. Five-year-olds were much more likely than nine-year-olds to assert incorrectly that the doll knew what animal it was.

Younger children showed the same kind of illusion of understanding that Piaget found when he asked children to interpret proverbs (see Chapter 3). Olson and Astington's study demonstrates the late development of the ability to distinguish what one sees (a color) from what one can know to be true (knowing what animal it is). Five- and six-year-olds did not acknowledge that they could see something and not know what it was, and that someone else could see something and not know. They did not realize that they were guessing and hence could be holding false beliefs. Olson and Astington argue that the failure to recognize beliefs as beliefs is what underlies childhood egocentrism and the inability to distinguish between appearance and reality. I suggest that this same failure underlies children's difficulty in understanding irony.

In Piaget and Inhelder's (1967) study of egocentrism, in which children were asked to decide how a scene appears to a doll at a vantage point different from their own, those younger than about six years of age tended to report their own view. Children's inappropriate attribution of their own knowledge to others is what is meant by egocentrism. But Olson and Astington's study suggests that children of this age *also* inappropriately attribute knowledge to themselves, knowledge which they cannot possibly have. Hence, perhaps the root of the problem is not difficulty in taking another's perspective (as Piaget believed) but rather difficulty in recognizing the distinction between seeing, believing, and external reality.

In studies by Flavell and his colleagues (Flavell, Flavell, and Green, 1983; Flavell and Taylor, 1984) of the appearance-reality distinction, children were shown odd objects, such as a sponge resembling a rock, and asked what they saw. Those who first said that it looked like a rock and who were then shown that it was actually a sponge, tended to switch their claim and say it looked like a sponge. Flavell calls this a realism error—the object is believed to resemble what it is known to be, even though there really is no resemblance. Olson and Astington suggest that the ability to distinguish appearance from reality rests on the ability to recognize that one might entertain a false belief about an object on the basis of its appearance. That is, one must be able to say to oneself: "I might believe that this object is a rock since it looks like one, but if so then I would be wrong." Or, "I once believed this was a rock but I was wrong." These findings correspond to those reported by Wimmer and Perner (1983; discussed in Chapter 8), who found that children younger than five or six years of age failed to attribute to a story character beliefs the children knew to be false. Taken together, the studies by Olson and Astington, Flavell and his colleagues, and Wimmer and Perner suggest that the child develops the ability to conceive of beliefs as potentially false, subjective mental events sometime around the age of six.

To understand the meaning underlying irony without the cue of intonation (which is often ignored by children or simply not given in the case of written statements), it is imperative to entertain questions about the speaker's beliefs. One must ask whether the speaker believes what he says (to rule out error) and whether he believes the hearer will believe what he says (to rule out lies). I suggest that children cannot understand irony much before age six precisely because they are unable to reflect about beliefs in this way until that age.

To understand the speaker meaning in metaphor, one need not entertain questions about beliefs. The question of whether the speaker believes what he says is not raised because an affirmative reply would be so implausible. Thus it is not surprising that we find comprehension and production of metaphor by children as young as three or four years old. The speaker meaning in metaphor requires only that the hearer have enough knowledge of the domains to which the topic and vehicle belong to discover the match between them.

Metaphor comprehension calls on the child to categorize objects in a new way, on the basis of similarity. This comes naturally to children. They cannot help doing this. Irony comprehension calls on the child to infer another's beliefs. And thinking about beliefs—one's own or others'—does not come naturally to children. A metacognitive ability, this mode of thinking does not emerge until sometime near the beginning of the school years.

Both metaphor and irony can be seen as manifestations of a more pervasive human ability—the capacity to perceive and communicate about things as other than they first appear. Although the capacity to recognize the here and now is present in animals generally, and the capacity to communicate about that state is found in higher animal species, only humans can imagine and communicate about other states: the past and the future, the probable and the improbable, what is and what is not. More generally, humans can grasp the true state of things even when appearances are deceptive.

This general and distinctive human ability manifests itself in various ways. It is this ability that enables the scientist to make inferences about unseen structures. This same ability is involved in art: the painter moves us with the physiognomy of a fictional face; the writer creates characters in a fictional world and expects us to derive truth and meaning from situations we know never occurred.

The ability to go beyond superficial appearances emerges in incipient forms in the first few years of life. Children sometimes pretend even before they speak. They feed imaginary food to their animals, lie down in make-believe sleep, and pretend to cry. And even in their early scribbles, children attempt representation. What looks like a meaningless line on a page becomes imbued with meaning—it is a car zooming along a road, an airplane flying, or a rabbit hopping.

The recognition that something is true on one level though false (or irrelevant) on a more superficial level is required by various forms of language—in indirect requests ("Would you mind closing the door?") in which the hearer must recognize that what is meant is different from what is said; in fiction, in which the reader must suspend disbelief; and in metaphor and irony, in which the hearer must recognize that what is meant is different from what is said and be able to derive meaning, perhaps even truth, from statements known to be false.

The ability to go beyond the given, and even to contradict the given, emerges early in rudimentary forms but takes its highest form in the discoveries of science and the worlds of art. It is the task of psychology to try to untangle the relationships among the many expressions of this ability. In this book I have sought to analyze this ability as it manifests itself in nonliteral language. What is astonishing is the prevalence of this ability, the many forms it takes, and the seeming inevitability of its emergence in the first few years of life.

References

Ackerman, B. 1981a. When is a question not answered? The understanding of young children of utterances violating or conforming
to the rules of conversational sequencing. *Journal of Experimental Child Psychology* 31: 487–507.

———— 1981b. Young children's understanding of a speaker's intentional use of a false utterance. *Developmental Psychology* 17:
472–480.

———— 1982. Contextual integration and utterance interpretation:
The ability of children and adults to interpret sarcastic utterances.
Child Development 53: 1075–83.

———— 1983a. Form and function in children's understanding of
ironic utterances. *Journal of Experimental Child Psychology* 35:
487–508.

———— 1983b. Speaker bias in children's evaluation of the external
consistency of statements. *Journal of Experimental Child Psychology* 35: 111–127.

———— 1985. Excuse inference modification in children and adults.
Journal of Experimental Child Psychology 39: 85–106.

Andrews, J., E. Rosenblatt, U. Malkus, H. Gardner, and E. Winner.
1986. Children's abilities to distinguish metaphoric and ironic
utterances from mistakes and lies. *Communication and Cognition* 19: 281–298.

Anglin, J. 1977. *Word, object, and conceptual development.* New
York: Norton.

Annett, M. 1959. The classification of instances of four common class
concepts by children and adults. *British Journal of Educational
Psychology* 29: 223–236.

Aristotle. 1952a. *Poetics*, trans. I. Bywater. In *The works of Aristotle,* vol. 11: *Rhetorical, De rhetorica ad Alexandrum, Poetica*, ed. W. D. Ross. Oxford: Clarendon Press.

—— 1952b. *Rhetoric*, trans. I. Bywater. In *The works of Aristotle*, vol. 11: *Rhetorical, De rhetorica ad Alexandrum, Poetica*, ed. W. D. Ross. Oxford: Clarendon Press.

Arter, J. 1976. The effects of metaphor on reading comprehension. Ph.D. diss., University of Illinois.

Asch, S. 1955. On the use of metaphor in the description of persons. In *On expressive language*, ed. H. Werner. Worcester: Clark University Press.

Asch, S., and H. Nerlove. 1960. The development of double function terms in children: An exploratory investigation. In *Perspectives in psychological theory: Essays in honor of Heinz Werner*, ed. B. Kaplan and S. Wapner. New York: International Universities Press.

Bach, K., and S. Harnish. 1979. *Linguistic communication and speech acts*. Cambridge, Mass.: MIT Press.

Barrett, M. 1978. Lexical development and overextension in child language. *Journal of Child Language* 5: 205–219.

Berg-Cross, L. 1975. Intentionality, degree of damage, and moral judgments. *Child Development* 46: 970–974.

Berndt, T., and E. Berndt. 1975. Children's use of motives and intentionality in person perception and moral judgment. *Child Development* 46: 904–912.

Billow, R. 1975. A cognitive-developmental study of metaphor comprehension. *Developmental Psychology* 11: 415–423.

—— 1981. Observing spontaneous metaphor in children. *Journal of Experimental Child Psychology* 31:430–445.

Black, M. 1962. *Models and metaphors*. Ithaca, N.Y.: Cornell University Press.

—— 1979. More about metaphor. In *Metaphor and thought*, ed. A. Ortony. New York: Cambridge University Press.

Bloom, L. 1973. *One word at a time*. The Hague: Mouton.

Boden, 1977. *Artificial intelligence and natural man*. New York: Basic Books.

Booth, W. 1974. *A rhetoric of irony*. Chicago: University of Chicago Press.

Bornstein, M. 1984. A descriptive taxonomy of psychological categories used by infants. In *Origins of cognitive skills*, ed. C. Sophian. Hillsdale, N.J.: Erlbaum.

Bornstein, M., W. Kessen, and S. Weiskopf. 1976. Color vision and hue categorization in young human infants. *Journal of Experi-*

mental Psychology: Human Perception and Performance 2: 115–129.

Bower, T. G. R. 1974. *Development in infancy.* San Francisco: W. H. Freeman.

Bowerman, M. 1976. Semantic factors in the acquisition of rules for word use and sentence construction. In *Normal and deficient child language,* ed. D. Morehead. Baltimore: University Park Press.

——— 1977. The acquisition of word meaning: An investigation of some current concepts. In *Thinking,* ed. P. Johnson-Laird and P. Wason. Cambridge: Cambridge University Press.

Bretherton, I., and M. Beeghly. 1982. Talking about internal states: The acquisition of an explicit theory of mind. *Developmental Psychology* 18: 906–921.

Broad, W. 1985. Subtle analogies found at the core of Edison's genius. *New York Times,* March 12, pp. C1–C2.

Brooke-Rose, C. 1958. *A grammar of metaphor.* London: Seeker and Warburg.

Brown, R. 1973. *A first language: The early stages.* Cambridge, Mass.: Harvard University Press.

Bruner, J., R. Olver, and P. Greenfield. 1966. *Studies in cognitive growth.* New York: Wiley.

Calhoun, A. 1984. The effects of perceptual, functional, and action based grounds on children's comprehension of metaphors. Paper no. 7, Language Research Group, Department of Psychology, University of North Carolina at Greensboro.

Carbonell, J. 1982. Metaphor: An inescapable phenomenon in natural-language comprehension. In *Strategies for natural language processing,* ed. W. Lehnert and M. Ringle. Hillsdale, N.J.: Erlbaum.

Carlson, P., and M. Anisfeld. 1969. Some observations on the linguistic competence of a two-year-old child. *Child Development* 40: 565–575.

Carnap, R. 1956. *Meaning and necessity,* 2nd ed. Chicago: University of Chicago Press.

Cassirer, E. 1946. *Language and myth.* New York: Dover.

Cerbin, W. 1985. Young children's comprehension of metaphoric language. Paper presented at the biennial meeting of the Society for Research in Child Development, Toronto.

Chandler, M., and S. Greenspan. 1972. Ersatz egocentrism: A reply to Borke. *Developmental Psychology* 7: 104–106.

Chomsky, N. 1965. *Aspects of the theory of syntax.* Cambridge, Mass.: MIT Press.

Chukovsky, K. 1968. *From two to five*. Berkeley: University of California Press.

Cicone, M., H. Gardner, and E. Winner. 1981. Understanding the psychology in psychological metaphors. *Journal of Child Language* 8: 213–216.

Clark, E. 1973. What's in a word? On the child's acquisition of semantics in his first language. In *Cognitive development and the acquisition of language,* ed. T. E. Moore. New York: Academic Press.

———— 1983. Meanings and concepts. In *Handbook of child psychology*, vol. 3: *Cognitive development,* ed. J. Flavell and E. Markman. New York: Wiley.

Clark, H., and R. Gerrig. 1984. On the pretense theory of irony. *Journal of Experimental Psychology: General* 113: 121–126.

Clark, H., and P. Lucy. 1975. Understanding what is meant from what is said: A study in conversationally conveyed requests. *Journal of Verbal Learning and Verbal Behavior* 14: 56–72.

Cohen, L. 1979. The semantics of metaphor. In *Metaphor and thought,* ed. A. Ortony. New York: Cambridge University Press.

Cometa, M., and M. Eson. 1978. Logical operations and metaphor interpretation: A Piagetian model. *Child Development* 49: 649–659.

Connor, K. 1983. Literal and figurative comparisons: Developmental patterns in preference for direction. Paper presented at the biennial meeting of the Society for Research in Child Development, Detroit.

Connor, K., and N. Kogan. 1980. Topic-vehicle relations in metaphor: the issue of asymmetry. In *Cognition and figurative language,* ed. R. P. Honeck and R. R. Hoffman. Hillsdale, N.J.: Erlbaum.

Connor, K., and A. Martin. 1982. Children's recognition of asymmetry in metaphor. Paper presented at the meeting of the Southeastern Conference on Human Development, Baltimore.

Conti, D., and L. Camras. 1984. Children's understanding of conversational principles. *Journal of Experimental Child Psychology* 38: 456–463.

Crisafi, M., and A. Brown. 1983. Flexible use of an inferential reasoning rule by very young children. Paper presented at the biennial meeting of the Society for Research in Child Development, Detroit.

Cutler, A. 1974. On saying what you mean without meaning what you say. In *Papers from the Tenth Regional Meeting, Chicago*

Linguistic Society. Chicago: Department of Linguistics, University of Chicago.

Damon, W. 1967. The child's conception of literary emotion. Honors thesis, Harvard College.

Dascal, M. 1981. Contextualism. In *Possibilities and limitations of pragmatics: Proceedings of the Conference on Pragmatics, Urbino, Italy, 1979,* ed. H. Parret, M. Sbisa, and J. Verschueren. Amsterdam: John Benjamins.

Davidson, D. 1979. On metaphor. In *On metaphor,* ed. S. Sachs. Chicago: University of Chicago Press.

——— 1984. Thought and talk. In *Inquiries into truth and interpretation,* ed. D. Davidson. New York: Oxford University Press.

DeLoache, J., M. Strauss, J. Maynard. 1979. Picture perception in infancy. *Infant Behavior and Development* 2: 77–89.

Demorest, A., L. Silberstein, H. Gardner, and E. Winner. 1983. Telling it as it isn't: Children's understanding of figurative language. *British Journal of Developmental Psychology* 1: 121–134.

Demorest, A., C. Meyer, E. Phelps, H. Gardner, and E. Winner. 1984. Words speak louder than actions: Understanding deliberately false remarks. *Child Development* 55: 1527–34.

Dent, C. 1984. The developmental importance of motion information in perceiving and describing metaphoric similarity. *Child Development* 55: 1607–13.

Dixon, K., A. Ortony, and D. Pearson. 1980. Some reflections on the use of figurative language in children's books. Paper presented at the National Reading Conference, San Diego.

Duncker, K. 1945. On problem solving. *Psychological Monographs* 58, no. 270.

Ekman, P. 1985. *Telling lies: Clues to deceit in the marketplace, politics, and marriage.* New York: Norton.

Elam, A. 1979. Metaphor: Its effects on the reading comprehension of sixth graders. Ph.D. diss., University of Georgia.

Elkind, D. 1969. Piagetian and psychometric conceptions of intelligence. *Harvard Educational Review* 39: 319–337.

——— 1974. *Children and adolescents: Interpretive essays on Jean Piaget.* New York: Oxford University Press.

——— 1976. *Child development and education: A Piagetian perspective.* New York: Oxford University Press.

Elkind, D., and R. Dabek. 1977. Personal injury and property damage in the moral judgments of children. *Child Development* 48: 276–289.

Flapan, D. 1968. *Children's understanding of social interaction.* New York: Columbia University Teacher's College Press.

Flavell, J. 1978. The development of knowledge about visual perception. In *Nebraska symposium on motivation,* vol. 25, ed. C. B. Keasey. Lincoln: University of Nebraska Press.

Flavell, J., and M. Taylor. 1984. Seeing and believing: Children's understanding of the distinction between appearance and reality. *Child Development* 55: 1710–20.

Flavell, J., E. Flavell, and F. Green. 1983. Development of the appearance-reality distinction. *Cognitive Psychology* 15: 95–120.

Flavell, J., S. Shipstead, and K. Croft. 1978. Young children's knowledge about visual perception: Hiding objects from others. *Child Development* 49: 1208–11.

Flavell, J., J. Speer, F. Green, and D. August. 1981. The development of comprehension monitoring and knowledge about communication. *Monographs of the Society for Research in Child Development* 46: 5, 192.

Flavell, J., P. Botkin, C. Fry, J. Wright, and P. Jarvis. 1968. *The development of role taking and communicative skills in children.* New York: Wiley.

Forster, K. 1981. Priming and the effects of sentence and lexical contexts on naming time: Evidence for autonomous lexical processing. *Quarterly Journal of Experimental Psychology* 33A: 465–495.

Fowler, H. 1965. *A dictionary of modern English usage,* 2nd ed. Oxford: Oxford University Press.

Frege, G. 1892. On sense and reference. In *Translations from the philosophical writings of Gottlob Frege,* ed. P. Greach and M. Black. Oxford: Oxford University Press, 1966.

Gardner, H. 1974. Metaphors and modalities: How children project polar adjectives onto diverse domains. *Child Development* 45: 84–91.

——— 1980. *Artful scribbles: The significance of children's drawings.* New York: Basic Books.

Gardner, H., and E. Winner. 1982. First intimations of artistry. In *U-shaped behavioral growth,* ed. S. Strauss. New York: Academic Press.

Gardner, H., M. Kircher, E. Winner, and D. Perkins. 1975. Children's metaphoric productions and preferences. *Journal of Child Language* 2: 125–141.

Gaus, P. 1979. The effects of three types of metaphor on sixth grade students' reading comprehension. Ph.D. diss., University of Arizona.

Gazdar, G. 1981. Speech act assignment. In *Elements of discourse understanding,* ed. A. Joshi, B. Webber, and I. Sag. Cambridge: Cambridge University Press.

Gelman, R., and R. Baillargeon. 1983. A review of some Piagetian concepts. In *Handbook of child psychology,* vol. 3: *Cognitive development.* New York: Wiley.

Gentner, D. 1977. Children's performances on a spatial analogies task. *Child Development* 48: 1034–39.

———— 1982. Are scientific analogies metaphors? In *Metaphor: Problems and perspectives,* ed. D. Miall. Brighton, East Sussex: Harvester Press.

———— 1983. Structure mapping: A theoretical framework for analogy. *Cognitive Science* 7: 155–170.

Gentner, D., and P. Stuart. 1983. Metaphor as structure mapping: What develops? Paper presented at the biennial meeting of the Society for Research in Child Development, Detroit.

Gibbs, R. 1979. Contextual effects in understanding indirect requests. *Discourse Processes* 2: 1–10.

———— 1980. Spilling the beans on understanding and memory for idioms in conversation. *Memory and Cognition* 8: 449–456.

———— 1982. A critical examination of the contribution of literal meaning to understanding nonliteral discourse. *Text* 2: 19–27.

———— 1984. Literal meaning and psychological theory. *Cognitive Science* 8: 275–304.

———— 1986. On the psycholinguistics of sarcasm. *Journal of Experimental Psychology: General* 115: 3–15.

Gick, M., and K. Holyoak. 1980. Analogical problem solving. *Cognitive Psychology* 12: 306–355.

Gildea, P., and S. Glucksberg. 1983. On understanding metaphor: The role of context. *Journal of Verbal Learning and Verbal Behavior* 22: 577–590.

Glucksberg, S. 1984. How people use context to resolve ambiguity: Implications for an interactive model of language understanding. In *Proceedings, International Conference on Knowledge and Language,* ed. J. Danks, I. Kurcz, and G. Shugar. Amsterdam: North Holland Press.

Glucksberg, S., P. Gildea, and H. Bookin. 1982. On understanding nonliteral speech: Can people ignore metaphors? *Journal of Verbal Learning and Verbal Behavior* 21: 85–98.

Glucksberg, S., R. Kreuz, and S. Rho. 1986. Context can constrain lexical access: Implications for models of language comprehension. *Journal of Experimental Psychology: Learning, Memory, and Cognition* 12: 323–335.

Goodman, N. 1976. *Languages of art*. Indianapolis: Hackett.

Gordon, D., and G. Lakoff. 1971. Conversational postulates. In *Papers from the Seventh Regional Meeting, Chicago Linguistic Society*. Chicago: Department of Linguistics, University of Chicago.

Gottfried, A., S. Rose, and W. Bridger. 1977. Cross-modal transfer in human infants. *Child Development* 48: 118–123.

Greene, R. 1982. Now you mean it—now you don't: An exploratory study of children's sensitivity to consistent and discrepant message meaning. Paper presented at the annual meeting of the Boston University Language Development Conference, Boston.

Grice, H. 1975. Logic and conversation. In *Syntax and semantics,* vol. 3: *Speech acts,* ed. P. Cole and J. Morgan. New York: Academic.

——— 1978. Some further notes on logic and conversation. In *Syntax and semantics,* vol. 9: *Pragmatics,* ed. P. Cole. New York: Academic.

Guillaume, P. 1927. Les débuts de la phrase dans le langage de l'enfant. *Journal de Psychologie* 24: 1–25.

Hanson, R. 1982. An investigation of the similarity and contrast models of metaphorical and categorical semantic processing. Ph.D. diss., Purdue University.

Harris, P., A. Kruithof, M. Terwogt, and T. Visser. 1981. Children's detection and awareness of textual anomaly. *Journal of Experimental Child Psychology* 31: 212–230.

Harris, R. 1976. Comprehension of metaphor: A test of a two-stage processing model. *Bulletin of the Psychonomic Society* 8: 321–324.

Harwood, D., and R. Verbrugge. 1977. Metaphor and the asymmetry of similarity. Paper presented at the annual meeting of the American Psychological Association, San Francisco.

Hayes, D., and R. Tierney. Developing readers' knowledge through analogy. *Reading Research Quarterly* 2: 256–280.

Hochberg, J., and V. Brooks. 1962. Pictorial recognition as an unlearned ability: A study of one child's performance. *American Journal of Psychology* 75: 624–628.

Hogrefe, G.-J., H. Wimmer, and J. Perner. 1986. Ignorance versus false belief: A developmental lag in attribution of epistemic states. *Child Development* 57: 567–582.

Holyoak, K., E. Junn, and D. Billman. 1984. Development of analogical problem solving skill. *Child Development* 55: 2042–55.

Honeck, R. P. 1980. Historical notes on figurative language. In *Cognition and figurative language,* ed. R. P. Honeck and R. R. Hoffman. Hillsdale, N.J.: Erlbaum.

Honeck, R. P., B. Sowry, and K. Voegtle. 1978. Proverbial understanding in a pictorial context. *Child Development* 49: 327–331.

Honeck, R. P., K. Voegtle, M. A. Dorfmueller, and R. R. Hoffman. 1980. Proverbs, meaning, and group structure. In *Cognition and figurative language,* ed. R. P. Honeck and R. R. Hoffman. Hillsdale, N.J.: Erlbaum.

Hudson, J., and K. Nelson. 1984. Play with language: Overextensions as analogies. *Journal of Child Language* 11: 337–346.

Inhelder, B., and J. Piaget. 1958. *The growth of logical thinking from childhood to adolescence.* New York: Basic Books.

——— 1964. *The early growth of logic in the child.* London: Routledge and Kegan Paul.

Johnson, J. 1982. The development of metaphor comprehension: Its mental-demand measurement and its process analytical models. Ph.D. diss., York University, Toronto.

Kaplan, J., E. Winner, and E. Rosenblatt. 1987. Children's abilities to discriminate and understand irony and metaphor. Unpublished research.

Kaplan, J., J. Levy, E. Rosenblatt, H. Gardner, and E. Winner. 1987. Sensitivity to the social functions of irony. Unpublished manuscript.

Karniol, R. 1978. Children's use of intention cues in evaluating behavior. *Psychological Bulletin* 85: 76–85.

Karttunen, L., and S. Peters. 1975. Conventional implicature in Montague grammar. Paper presented at the first annual meeting of the Berkeley Linguistic Society, University of California, Berkeley.

Katz, A. 1982. Metaphoric relationships: The role of feature saliency. *Journal of Psycholinguistic Research* 11: 283–296.

Katz, J. 1981. Literal meaning and logical theory. *Journal of Philosophy* 78: 203–234.

Katz, J., and J. Fodor. 1963. The structure of semantic theory. *Language* 39: 170–210.

Kaufer, D. 1981. Understanding ironic communication. *Journal of Pragmatics* 5: 495–510.

Keil, F. 1979. *Semantic and conceptual development.* Cambridge, Mass.: Harvard University Press.

———— 1985. Semantic fields and the acquisition of metaphor. Unpublished manuscript.

Kelly, M., and F. Keil. 1984. Metaphor comprehension and knowledge of semantic domains. Paper presented at the annual meeting of American Psychological Association, Toronto.

Kiger, J., and A. Glass. 1983. The facilitation of lexical decisions by a prime occurring after the target. *Memory and Cognition* 11: 356–365.

Kittay, E., and A. Lehrer. 1981. Semantic fields and the structure of metaphor. *Studies in Language* 5: 31–63.

Koch, K. 1970. *Wishes, lies and dreams.* New York: Chelsea House.

Kogan, N., K. Connor, A. Gross, and D. Fava. 1980. Understanding visual metaphor: Developmental and individual differences. *Monographs of the Society for Research in Child Development* 45: 1.

Koriat, A. 1981. Semantic facilitation in lexical decision as a function of prime-target association. *Memory and Cognition* 9: 587–598.

Lakoff, G., and M. Johnson. 1980. *Metaphors we live by.* Chicago: University of Chicago Press.

Lempers, J., E. Flavell, and J. Flavell. 1977. The development in very young children of tacit knowledge concerning visual perception. *Genetic Psychology Monographs* 95: 3–53.

Lesser, H., and C. Drouin. 1975. Training in the use of double-function terms. *Journal of Psycholinguistic Research* 4: 285–302.

Lewkowicz, D., and G. Turkewitz. 1980. Cross-modal equivalence in early infancy: Auditory-visual intensity matching. *Developmental Psychology* 16: 597–607.

MacCormac, E. 1985. *A cognitive theory of metaphor.* Cambridge, Mass.: Bradford Books.

Marjanovic, A. 1983. Criteria of metaphoricity of children's utterances. Paper presented at the annual meeting of the American Psychological Association, Anaheim, California.

Markman, E. 1977. Realizing that you don't understand: A preliminary investigation. *Child Development* 48: 986–992.

———— 1979. Realizing that you don't understand: Elementary school children's awareness of inconsistencies. *Child Development* 50: 643–655.

Markman, E., and J. Hutchinson. 1984. Children's sensitivity to constraints on word meaning: Taxonomic vs. thematic relations. *Cognitive Psychology* 16: 1–27.

Marks, L. 1975. On colored-hearing synesthesia: Cross-modal translations of sensory dimensions. *Psychological Bulletin* 82: 303–331.

———— 1978. *The unity of the senses: Interrelations among the modalities*. New York: Academic Press.

———— 1982a. Bright sneezes and dark coughs, loud sunlight and soft moonlight. *Journal of Experimental Psychology: Human Perception and Performance* 8: 177–193.

———— 1982b. Synesthetic perception and poetic metaphor. *Journal of Experimental Psychology: Human Perception and Performance* 8: 15–23.

Marks, L., and Bornstein, M. 1985. Sensory similarities: Classes, characteristics, and cognitive consequences. In *Cognition and symbolic structures: The psychology of metaphoric transformation*, ed. R. E. Haskell. Norwood, N.J.: Ablex.

Marks, L., and R. Hammeal. 1981. Does brightness mean loudness or pitch to children? Paper presented at the annual meeting of the Psychonomic Society, Philadelphia.

Marks, L., R. Hammeal, and M. Bornstein. In press. Children's comprehension of cross-modal similarity: Perception and metaphor. In *Monographs of the Society for Research in Child Development*.

Marti, E. 1979. La pensée analogique chez l'enfant de 2 à 7 ans. Ph.D. diss., University of Geneva.

Marvin, R., M. Greenberg, and D. Mossler. 1976. The early development of conceptual perspective taking: Distinguishing among multiple perspectives. *Child Development* 47: 511–514.

McCarthy, M., E. Winner, and H. Gardner. 1980. The ontogenesis of metaphor. In *Cognition and figurative language*, ed. R. P. Honeck and R. R. Hoffman. Hillsdale, N.J.: Erlbaum.

Mendelsohn, E., H. Gardner, and E. Winner. 1981. A study of children's perception of metaphoric grounds. Unpublished research.

Mendelsohn, E., E. Winner, and H. Gardner. 1980. The spontaneous production of analogies by grade school children. Technical Report no. 13, Project Zero, Harvard University.

Mendelsohn, E., S. Robinson, H. Gardner, and E. Winner. 1984. Are preschoolers' renamings intentional category violations? *Developmental Psychology* 20: 187–192.

Miller, G. 1979. Images and models, similes and metaphors. In *Metaphor and thought*, ed. A. Ortony. New York: Cambridge University Press.

Miller, G., and P. Johnson-Laird. 1976. *Language and perception*. Cambridge: Cambridge University Press.

Miller, P. 1985. Children's reasoning about the causes of human behavior. *Journal of Experimental Child Psychology* 39: 343–362.

Moore, B. 1986. An example of a young child's use of a physical-psychological metaphor. Unpublished paper.

Mossler, D., R. Marvin, and M. Greenberg. 1976. Conceptual perspective taking in 2- to 6-year-old children. *Developmental Psychology* 12: 85–86.

Nelson, K. 1974. Concept, word and sentence: Interrelations in acquisition and development. *Psychological Review* 81: 267–285.

Nelson, K., L. Rescorla, J. Gruendel, and H. Benedict. 1978. Early lexicons: What do they mean? *Child Development* 49: 960–968.

Nippold, M., L. Leonard, and R. Kail. 1984. Syntactic and conceptual factors in children's understanding of metaphors. *Journal of Speech and Hearing Research* 27: 197–205.

Olson, D. 1977. From utterance to text: The bias of language in speech and writing. *Harvard Educational Review* 47: 257–281.

—— 1986. Or what's a metaphor? Unpublished manuscript.

Olson, D., and J. Astington. 1987. Seeing and knowing: On the ascription of mental states to young children. *Canadian Journal of Psychology* 41, no. 4: 399–411.

Olson, D., and A. Hildyard. 1983. Literacy and the comprehension and expression of literal meaning. In *Writing in Focus,* ed. F. Coulmas and K. Ehrlich. New York: Mouton, pp. 291–325.

Onifer, W., and D. Swinney. 1981. Accessing lexical ambiguities during sentence comprehension: Effects of frequency of meaning and contextual bias. *Memory and Cognition* 9: 225–236.

Ortony, A. 1975. Why metaphors are necessary and not just nice. *Educational Theory* 25: 45–53.

—— 1979a. Beyond literal similarity. *Psychological Review* 86: 161–180.

Ortony, A., ed. 1979b. *Metaphor and thought.* New York: Cambridge University Press.

Ortony, A., R. Reynolds, and J. Arter. 1978. Metaphor: Theoretical and empirical research. *Psychological Bulletin* 85: 919–943.

Ortony, A., R. Vondruska, M. Foss, and L. Jones. 1985. Salience, similes and the asymmetry of similarity. *Journal of Memory and Language* 24: 569–594.

Osborn, M., and D. Ehninger. 1962. The metaphor in public address. *Speech Monographs* 29: 223–234.

Osgood, C., G. Suci, and P. Tannenbaum. 1957. *The measurement of meaning.* Urbana: University of Illinois Press.

Patterson, C., D. Massad, and J. Cosgrove. 1978. Children's referential communication: Component plans for effective listening. *Developmental Psychology* 14: 401–406.

Pearson, P., R. Raphael, H. Hyser, and R. TePaske. 1981. The function of metaphor in children's recall of expository passages. *Journal of Reading Behavior* 13: 249–261.

Perner, J., and H. Wimmer. 1985. "John *thinks* that Mary *thinks* that . . .": Attribution of second-order beliefs by 5- to 10-year-old children. *Journal of Experimental Child Psychology* 39: 437–471.

Perner, J., S. Leekam, and H. Wimmer. 1984. The insincerity of conservation questions: Children's growing sensitivity to experimenter's epistemic intention. Unpublished manuscript.

Piaget, J. 1929. *The child's conception of the world.* New York: Harcourt, Brace.

——— 1932. *The moral judgment of the child.* New York: Harcourt, Brace.

——— 1962. *Play, dreams and imitation in childhood.* New York: Norton.

——— 1974. *The language and thought of the child.* New York: New American Library.

Piaget, J., and B. Inhelder. 1967. *The child's conception of space.* New York: Norton.

Pickens, J., and H. Pollio. 1979. Patterns of figurative language competence in adult speakers. *Psychological Research* 40: 299–313.

Pollio, M. 1973. The development and augmentation of figurative language. Ph.D. diss., University of Tennessee.

Pollio, M., and J. Pickens. 1980. The developmental structure of figurative competence. In *Cognition and figurative language,* ed. R. P. Honeck and R. R. Hoffman. Hillsdale, N.J.: Erlbaum.

Pollio, M., and H. Pollio. 1974. The development of figurative language in school children. *Journal of Psycholinguistic Research* 3: 185–201.

Reich, P. 1976. The early acquisition of word meaning. *Journal of Child Language* 3: 117–123.

Rescorla, L. 1980. Overextension in early language development. *Journal of Child Language* 7: 321–335.

Reynolds, R., and A. Ortony. 1980. Some issues in the measurement of children's comprehension of metaphorical language. *Child Development* 51: 1110–19.

Ricciuti, H. 1965. Object grouping and selective ordering in infants 12–24 months old. *Merrill Palmer Quarterly* 11: 129–148.

Richards, I. A. 1936. *The philosophy of rhetoric.* London: Oxford University Press.

Rosch, E. 1973. Natural categories. *Cognitive Psychology* 4: 328–350.

——— 1975. Cognitive reference points. *Cognitive Psychology* 7: 532–547.

Rosch, E., C. Mervis, W. Gray, D. Johnson, and P. Boyes-Braem. 1976. Basic objects in natural categories. *Cognitive Psychology* 8: 382–439.

Rosenblatt, E., D. Swinney, H. Gardner, and E. Winner. 1987. On-line processing of metaphor and irony. Unpublished research.

Ross, G. 1980. Categorization in 1- to 2-year-olds. *Developmental Psychology* 16: 391–396.

Rubin, S., and H. Gardner. 1985. Once upon a time: The development of sensitivity to story structure. In *Researching response to literature and the teaching of literature: Points of departure*, ed. C. Cooper. Norwood, N.J.: Ablex.

Rumelhart, D. 1979. Some problems with the notion of literal meanings. In *Metaphor and thought*, ed. A. Ortony. New York: Cambridge University Press.

Rumelhart, D., and D. Norman. 1981. Analogical processes in learning. In *Cognitive skills and their acquisition*, ed. J. Anderson. Hillsdale, N.J.: Erlbaum.

Saddock, J. 1979. Figurative speech and linguistics. In *Metaphor and thought*, ed. A. Ortony. New York: Cambridge University Press.

Schiffer, S. 1972. *Meaning*. Oxford: Oxford University Press.

Schustack, M., and J. Anderson. 1979. Effects of analogy to prior knowledge on memory for new information. *Journal of Verbal Learning and Verbal Behavior* 18: 565–583.

Searle, J. 1979a. Literal meaning. In *Expression and meaning*, ed. J. Searle. Cambridge: Cambridge University Press.

——— 1979b. Metaphor. In *Metaphor and thought*, ed. A. Ortony. New York: Cambridge University Press.

Seidenberg, M., G. Waters, M. Sanders, and P. Langer. 1984. Pre- and post-lexical loci of contextual effects on word recognition. *Memory and Cognition* 12: 315–328.

Shantiris, K. 1983. Developmental changes in metaphor comprehension: It's not all uphill. Paper presented at the biennial meeting of the Society for Research in Child Development, Detroit.

Shatz, M., H. Wellman, and S. Silber. 1983. The acquisition of mental verbs: A systematic investigation of the first reference to mental state. *Cognition* 14: 301–321.

Shultz, T., and K. Cloghesy. 1981. Development of recursive awareness of intention. *Developmental Psychology* 17: 465–471.

Shultz, T., and F. Shamash. 1981. The child's conception of intending act and consequence. *Canadian Journal of Behavioural Science* 13: 368–372.

Schultz, T., D. Wells, and M. Sarda. 1980. The development of the ability to distinguish intended actions from mistakes, reflexes, and passive movements. *The British Journal of Social and Clinical Psychology* 19: 301–310.

Silverman, J., E. Winner, A. Rosensteil, and H. Gardner. 1975. On training sensitivity to painting styles. *Perception* 4: 373–384.

Simpson, G. 1981. Meaning dominance and semantic context in the processing of lexical ambiguity. *Journal of Verbal Learning and Verbal Behavior* 20: 120–136.

——— 1984. Lexical ambiguity and its role in models of word recognition. *Psychological Bulletin* 96: 316–340.

Skinner, B. F. 1957. *Verbal behavior.* New York: Appleton-Century Crofts.

Smith, M. 1978. Cognizing the behavior stream: The recognition of intentional action. *Child Development* 49: 736–743.

Snyder, J. 1979. The spontaneous production of figurative language and word play in the grade school years. Ph.D. diss., Boston University.

Spelke, E. 1976. Infants' intermodal perception of events. *Cognitive Psychology* 8: 553–560.

Sperber, D. 1984. Verbal irony: Pretense or echoic mention. *Journal of Experimental Psychology: General* 113: 130-136.

Swinney, D., and A. Cutler. 1979. The access and processing of idiomatic expressions. *Journal of Verbal Learning and Verbal Behavior* 18: 523–534.

Thomson, J., and R. Chapman. 1977. Who is "Daddy" revisited: The status of two-year-olds' overextended words in use and comprehension. *Journal of Child Language* 4: 359–375.

Tourangeau, R., and R. Sternberg. 1981. Aptness in metaphor. *Cognitive Psychology* 13: 27–55.

Turbayne, C. 1970. *The myth of metaphor,* rev. ed. Columbia: University of South Carolina Press.

Tversky, A. 1977. Features of similarity. *Psychological Review* 84: 327–352.

Verbrugge, R. 1977. Resemblances in language and perception. In *Perceiving, acting, and knowing,* ed. R. Shaw and J. Bransford. Hillsdale, N.J.: Erlbaum.

——— 1980. Transformations in knowing: A realist view of metaphor. In *Cognition and figurative languages,* ed. R. P. Honeck and R. R. Hoffman. Hillsdale, N.J.: Erlbaum.

Verbrugge, R., and N. McCarrell. 1977. Metaphoric comprehension: Studies in reminding and resembling. *Cognitive Psychology* 9: 494–533.

Vosniadou, S. 1987. Children and metaphors. *Child Development* 58: 870–885.

Vosniadou, S., and A. Ortony. 1983a. The emergence of the literal-metaphorical-anomalous distinction in young children. *Child Development* 54: 154–161.

—— 1983b. The influence of analogy in children's acquisition of new information from text: An exploratory study. In *Searches for meaning in reading, language processing, and instruction,* ed. J. Niles. Rochester, N.Y.: National Reading Conference.

—— 1986. Testing the metaphoric competence of the young child: Paraphrase vs. enactment. *Human Development* 29: 226–230.

Vosniadou, S., A. Ortony, R. Reynolds, and P. Wilson. 1984. Sources of difficulty in children's understanding of metaphorical language. *Child Development* 55: 1588–1606.

Vygotsky, L. 1962. *Thought and language.* Cambridge, Mass.: MIT Press.

Wagner, S., E. Winner, D. Cicchetti, and H. Gardner. 1981. "Metaphorical" mapping in human infants. *Child Development* 52: 728–731.

Wagner, S., E. Winner, H. Gardner, and D. Cicchetti. 1982. A heart-rate habituation study of auditory-visual matching in six-month-olds. Paper presented at the International Conference on Infant Studies, Austin, Texas.

Wason, P., and P. Johnson-Laird. 1972. *Psychology of reasoning: Structure and content.* Cambridge, Mass.: Harvard University Press.

Wellman, H., and D. Estes. 1984. Children's early use of mental verbs and what they mean. Paper presented at the annual meeting of the American Psychological Association, Toronto.

Wimmer, H., and J. Perner. 1983. Beliefs about beliefs: Representation and constraining function of wrong beliefs in young children's understanding of deception. *Cognition* 13: 103–128.

Wimmer, H., S. Gruber, and J. Perner. 1984. Young children's conception of lying: Lexical realism—moral subjectivism. *Journal of Experimental Child Psychology* 37: 1–30.

Winner, E. 1979. New names for old things: The emergence of metaphoric language. *Journal of Child Language* 6: 469–491.

—— 1982. *Invented worlds: The psychology of the arts.* Cambridge, Mass.: Harvard University Press.

Winner, E., and E. Gallagher. 1983. The role of behavioral and intonational cues in the understanding of irony. Unpublished manuscript.

Winner, E., and H. Gardner. 1977. The comprehension of metaphor in brain-damaged patients. *Brain* 100: 719–727.

———— 1978. A pictorial test of metaphor comprehension. Unpublished research.

Winner, E., M. Engel, and H. Gardner. 1980. Misunderstanding metaphor: What's the problem? *Journal of Experimental Child Psychology* 30: 22–32.

Winner, E., M. McCarthy, and H. Gardner. 1980. The ontogenesis of metaphor. In *Cognition and figurative language,* ed. R. P. Honeck and R. R. Hoffman. Hillsdale, N.J.: Erlbaum.

Winner, E., A. Rosenstiel, and H. Gardner. 1976. The development of metaphoric understanding. *Developmental Psychology* 12: 289–297.

Winner, E., M. Erwin, M. Joyce, and K. Kennedy. 1986. The role of identification in children's understanding of irony. Unpublished manuscript.

Winner, E., M. McCarthy, S. Kleinman, and H. Gardner. 1979. First metaphors. *New Directions for Child Development* 3: 29–42.

Winner, E., W. Wapner, M. Cicone, and H. Gardner. 1979. Measures of metaphor. *New Directions for Child Development* 6: 67–75.

Winner, E., G. Windmueller, E. Rosenblatt, L. Bosco, and E. Best. 1987. Making sense of literal and nonliteral falsehood. *Metaphor and Symbolic Processes* 2: 13–32.

Wolf, D., and H. Gardner. In preparation. *The making of meanings.*

Index